M000087142

The Marketing Mystique

Revised Edition

Edward S. McKay

Revised by
Arthur M. Rittenberg

American Management Association

New York • Atlanta • Boston • Chicago • Kansas City • San Francisco • Washington, D.C.
Brussels • Toronto • Mexico City • Tokyo

This publication is designed to provide accurate and authoritative information in regard to the subject matter covered. It is sold with the
understanding that the publisher is not engaged in rendering legal,
accounting, or other professional service. If legal advice or other expert assistance is required, the services of a competent professional
person should be sought.

Library of Congress Cataloging-in-Publication Data

McKay, Edward S.
    The marketing mystique / Edward S. McKay ; revised by Arthur M.
  Rittenberg.
        p.   cm.
    Includes bibliographical references and index.
    ISBN 0-8144-7808-5
    1. Marketing.   2. Marketing—Management.   I. Rittenberg, Arthur
  M.   II. Title.
  HF5415.M2585   1994
  658.8—dc20   93-27966
                                                              CIP

Printing number

10   9   8   7   6   5   4   3   2   1

Contents

Preface

Those of you in business or nonprofit organizations who find yourselves dealing with the marketing function and marketing people will find *The Marketing Mystique* a very useful tool.

Over the years, marketing people have developed something of a special language. As with any collection of jargon, there are at least two functions for this special language. The first is to effect a shorthand for discussions among one's peers. The second, however, may be to bar outsiders from meaningful discussion or knowledgeable involvement in some marketing matters. Jargon also permits presenting some old wine in new bottles.

The Marketing Mystique is designed to demystify marketing for all readers who desire to understand and practice the intricacies of the fascinating field of marketing. In today's market society, almost no one in business or nonprofits can afford to be excluded from marketing discussions or decisions.

The Marketing Mystique was first published in 1972. Publishing aficionados know that longevity of that order is most unusual in the genre of business books. This book has attained a loyal following among business executives who have read it and then recommended it to their colleagues.

For a book to survive that long and continue to sell to its constituency, it must have brought unique assets to its readers. The original author, Edward McKay, is the primary among these unique assets. While I never met him, I can say that the man, his training and expertise, his clarity of thought and expression, and his enviable grasp of the discipline of marketing shine forth on every page of the original book. I have regularly found myself marveling at the timelessness of Mr. McKay's philosophy, structure, and applications.

Mr. McKay defined the marketing concept in wonderfully concise terms. Well stated in its full form in Chapter 3, this is the marketing concept in brief:

> The purpose of marketing is to direct all aspects of the company to the needs and standards of the marketplace and to direct all marketing activities to the objectives of the business enterprise.

The Marketing Mystique can be a deskside reference for every business professional. Its checklists of marketing activities, scope, and purpose statements and its keen explication of the dimensions and ramifications of marketing will be regularly used by its readers.

The Marketing Mystique will also be of great value to those who must interface with marketing people and their plans and programs. The myriad executives whose work is daily impacted by the marketing function and marketing people will benefit from McKay's marvelous grasp of marketing and its relationship to all aspects of a dynamic organization.

Marketing people themselves will refer frequently to the clear and complete explanations and checklists of activities, cautions and sequences as they work their way through the demanding tasks and evaluations they regularly conduct.

—Arthur M. Rittenberg

Acknowledgments

I am obliged and delighted to mention the contributions of the AMACOM people who awarded me this demanding assignment, and who then worked with me to its completion: Weldon Rackley, director of AMACOM Books; Adrienne Hickey, senior editor; Ada Connors, senior editorial assistant; Richard Gatjens, associate editor; Thomas Finnegan, copy editor; Steve Arkin, director of marketing and sales, and all of the other AMACOM professionals who have contributed to this book's past and future successes. My thanks go to them all.

To Marge Maio Capone, who for so many years has been a professional right hand and who suffered through the torturous process of preparing the manuscript, go my thanks and appreciation.

To my family goes acknowledgment of their wonderful support and assistance throughout the vicissitudes of a fulfilling career. Cindy has proven to be a marketer of substantial skill and persistence and the best sales person we have. Gerry has already attained the heights of accomplishment and competency in his industry and is an acknowledged master of marketing's intricacies. Margie is clearly the best writer in the family and, if she had less pure talent, could be a marketer of note. Nes has proven the results of caring and dedication to the mastery of a profession. Carl has demonstrated that persistence and tenacity, coupled with a seize-the-moment attitude, will always win in marketing. And Linda has only temporarily retired from the marketing arena but will surely return to display her prodigious design and promotion skills.

To my six grandsons, Greg, Keith, Andy, James, Craig, and Garrett, who never fail to challenge my communications skills and to test my depth of commitment, go hopes for their futures.

Last and not least at all, to Louise, who has been there for a lifetime and who has disciplined me when I needed it, praised me when I deserved it, and settled my feet back on the ground when I tended to soar too high, go love, appreciation, and acknowledgment that it has been worth every step on the path of life with her.

—Arthur M. Rittenberg

Part One

Establishing a Market-Oriented Philosophy

1

Business: What's It All About?

The question has been asked many times: "What is the purpose of a business?" Many answers have been offered, such as:

"The purpose of a business is to make a profit."

"The purpose of a business is to reward the shareholders for their investment."

"The purpose of a business is to provide employment and stability for its owners and employees."

"The purpose of a business is to make a quality product or to provide quality service."

All of these are true. But then again, none of them is completely true. The answer, modified to meet the exigencies and needs of the end of the twentieth century, has to be:

"The purpose of a business is to find a problem, a need, or a want and to solve that situation by providing a product or service to a buyer who needs or wants it."

Elaborations and extensions to the answer may be necessary:

We have to provide that solution in a timely fashion, at a competitive price, and with appropriate support to the customer.

Of course, many such refinements and elaborations can be added. In fact, we will deal with a number of them in this book.

Marketing has the prime responsibility for, or at least a principle role in, carrying out all phases of our definition of a business. Look again at each element in the definition and notice the role that marketing has to play.

- Finding a problem or a need is a primary task of market research.
- In determining a solution to the problem, marketing brings to bear its knowledge of competition and its awareness of how the buyer will perceive the solution, that is, our product or service.

It is marketing that determines and communicates to the rest of the company what the definition of *timely* is from the customer's perspective. And it is marketing that determines and communicates the level, frequency, and manner of support that the customer will require.

Marketing is that aspect of a business that maintains an outward focus, that constantly has the customer in its eye. Most of the other functions of a business focus inwardly much of the time, including:

- Finance
- Manufacturing
- Legal
- Accounting
- Administrative services
- Information services
- Human resources
- Warehousing and fulfillment

To say that marketing focuses outwardly on the customer's needs and concerns while much else of business operations focuses inwardly on company concerns is not intended to be a criticism or a diminution of those operations' responsibility, authority, or contribution to company welfare.

Not at all. It is our intent only to establish the place and position of marketing in most business endeavors.

Once we understand the explicit role and positioning of marketing in a business organization, we can go on to further define the agenda that marketing carries within the organization.

Marketing is an agglomeration of a number of functions and activities in the business organization. The term *marketing* encompasses the following functions:

- Sales and sales management
- Advertising
- Sales promotion
- Publicity and public relations
- Market research
- Direct marketing
  - —Direct mail
  - —Telemarketing
  - —Coupon advertising
- Warehousing
- Transportation

This is not to say that in every organization all of these functions necessarily report to the marketing department. They often do not. We are saying that the term *marketing* encompasses all of these activities, and that they are a primary concern and of significant interest to marketing because these several functions can and do closely impact the primary mission of marketing.

That mission needs to be defined. The mission of marketing within a business organization is:

1. To determine customer needs
2. To determine the customer's criteria for filling those needs
3. To be aware of competitive activities and products, including but not limited to
   - Product changes
   - Product innovation

- Pricing
- Packaging
- Sales activities
- Promotional plans
- Advertising programs

4. To be aware of, and communicate to all interested and involved parties within the company, the legal and regulatory implications for its business and its products and services
5. To carry the primary responsibility for the movement of the company's products and services to its customers
6. To create and manage the budgets for costs related to the movement of products and services
7. To control costs in the marketing operation so as to maximize profits in the company's overall business activities

2

What Marketing Does

An old saying tells us to build a better mousetrap and the world will beat a path to our door.

Quite true, we say, but only under the following conditions:

1. If the world ever gets to hear about it
2. If consumers understand what our mousetrap is and what it does
3. If consumers understand why they need our mousetrap
4. If it is clear what our mousetrap's advantages are
5. If it is priced properly and competitively
6. If it is in the right place where our customers shop
7. If it is stocked in adequate quantities
8. If it has advantages over its competition
9. If the public understands and agrees with the superiority of our mousetrap
10. If there are no legal or regulatory problems with the use and installation of our mousetrap

Remember, only if we have all ten of these "ifs" in place do we have a good chance of having the world beat a path to our door.

Do you recognize all of these tasks as the province and concern of marketing? These are the things that marketing is charged with carrying out. If marketing is not actually responsible for doing all of them, it is still concerned that all be done and done well, and in a timely fashion.

We are defining marketing in terms of what it does and what it is concerned with. Let's remember that marketing is focused on moving the company's goods and services to the marketplace, and on informing and motivating a potential buyer to purchase them.

Marketing is dynamic, so much so that nothing that marketing does ever seems to be of a static nature. Marketing is always concerned with changing things. Marketing wants to change the nature of the market for its product or service, change the perception of its product or service, change the level of acceptance of its output, and change the position of competition in the marketplace.

In a 1991 review of markets and product capacity on a worldwide basis, *The Wall Street Journal* uses the headline "Glutted Markets" to describe a situation it further describes in its subheadline: "A Global Overcapacity Hurts Many Industries."

We submit that this so-called overcapacity must be seen for what it truly is: underdistribution and possibly overpricing. With so many markets throughout the major part of the world remaining yet to be developed, with so many people yet to be reached by marketers, we are not nearly ready for the *Journal's* elitist analysis of its limited view of the global marketplace.

There are literally billions of people on this globe who are underserved in numerous ways. They are underfed, underemployed, undersheltered, undermedicated, undertransported, and undereducated.

These markets are not glutted; these countries are certainly not overcapacitied.

Marketers must be people of vision or else they cannot be marketers. If they are not visionary, then they are reduced to being merely rearward-looking, measuring only what is and what was, not bothering with what ought to be, what might be, what must be.

3

Resolving the
Marketing Paradox

Ask any general manager, marketing manager, or sales manager about the philosophy of the business and you will be given an answer that probably makes some commitment to a customer orientation. They will tell you that they intend the organization to be customer-oriented.

Such commitments have become commonplace. Yet, we have a bewildering paradox in business today. Never have we heard so many complaints about business firms failing to serve their customers properly.

There is an almost universal sentiment that product quality, performance, and service are poor. There is grumbling about packaging, labeling, and pricing. Complaints are widespread about the quality and attentiveness of sales personnel.

There is persistent demand for government intervention and legislation to protect consumers from misinformation and fraud. There appears to be a substantial gap between the company's view of its focus, intent, and priorities and the same perceptions held by its customers. This can be viewed as a paradox.

We do not disagree with management's view of its philosophy. But when we listen to the customers' evaluations, we must take issue with management's *implementation* of its philosophy.

This gap between perception and reality must be bridged,

and we must look to marketing in its several activities to do this bridging so as to eliminate the paradox.

As a lead into the formulation of this approach, it is useful to review briefly the history and evolution of the marketing concept.

What Is the Marketing Concept?

As it has evolved over the last forty years, the marketing concept has had a wide variety of interpretations. It has also had its antagonists and critics.

First, the marketing concept in a particular company owes its being and definition to the philosophy of the company. That is:

- How the company views itself and its purpose
- How it views its products and services
- How it views its customers and its competition
- How it views its responsibility to its society

This concept can and does change. Some would hold that it must adapt in concert with changes in society and in the marketplace.

In the early stages of evolution of the marketing concept, the emphasis was on organization. In many cases, the implementation of the marketing concept meant simply that the sales manager's title was changed to marketing manager. In others, additional responsibilities were also added, such as market research. Advertising was incorporated into the sales department to form the new marketing department. No surprises, no miracles, not even any substantial changes occurred because of these changes.

In phase two of the development of the concept, organizations effected changes that were deeper and more substantive. These organizations chose to integrate all of the functions that focused on the customers' needs in order to serve them more effectively. The dictum that "The customer is king" was introduced.

The problem encountered here was that the customer did not always know what he or she wanted. Moreover, engineering and manufacturing could not always quickly adapt their operations to change. Finance would not always cope with these new demands, and conflict would often develop among the functions involved. No one argued against the customer-satisfaction focus, but the focus alone was not always enough to overcome real problems of implementation.

In the third phase of development of the concept, the new marketing function was given some authority and responsibility over decisions on products to be offered, production schedules and timing, pricing, and the sales appeal to be made.

This "marketing strategy" approach saw the marketing department moving into a position of leadership within the company in formulating strategy to provide competitive advantage in the marketplace.

The Five Levels of Customer Relationships

According to Philip Kotler

1. *Bare Bones Marketing*—in which the salesperson doesn't do anything but shake the customer's hand and say, "Thanks."
2. *Reactive Marketing*—in which the salesperson says to the customer, "If anything goes wrong, please call me."
3. *Accountability*—where the firm calls buyers a week or two after the sale to find out how the products are working and how satisfied they are. "Is there anything about the product that can be improved upon?" is a good way to gather ideas for improvement.
4. *Show Continued Interest*—means calling customers and telling them how to get better use out of the product even long after the sale has been made.
5. *Real Partnership*—means becoming a partner with the customer in actually codesigning the product and researching how both parties can gain in the process of working together.

Source: A speech at an American Marketing Association meeting, reported in *Marketing News* (June 8, 1992), a publication of the AMA.

These developments were followed by the implementation of a "systems" approach to marketing. The terms *systems analysis and synthesis* and *operations research* were introduced, and the use of the computer was upon us. Marketing games, simulations, modeling, decision trees, program evaluation and review technique (PERT), and other new and, at that time, trendy tools were brought to bear.

The use of the computer in storing, compiling, and manipulating data has had and will continue to have tremendous impact on marketing. Analysis of data on demographics, pricing, consumer-selection processes, competitive market share, and similar information stored in electronic databases provides tremendous opportunities to the marketer who seeks more information on which to base marketing decisions.

However, let us not mistake information or data for decisions. We are still, and it appears we will always be, in a mode where it is the interpreter of the data, not the compiler of it, whose judgment will be sought and valued. Marketing decisions and strategy making are still human events.

The Luddites of the Industrial Revolution in England, protesting the advent of the machine age because it threatened their existence and livelihood, wrecked the laborsaving machinery that would cause their unemployment. We do not advocate a modern Luddite expedition against the computer; quite the reverse. We suggest harnessing the computer to our needs for compiling data and massaging and manipulating it, but never permitting the data to speak for itself.

More than ever before, marketing people will need to look to the fundamentals of their craft to make important decisions for their companies. As marketers use it, the term *strategy* is not synonymous with data. It means judgment based on the data, along with acquired experience and learned intuition.

We are pursuing a definition of the marketing concept in a five-part framework:

1. A business philosophy
2. An organizational form for marketing
3. An approach to strategic planning

4. A dynamic operating system
5. A means of performance appraisal

Socrates once told a young man, "By all means marry. If you get a good wife you will be very happy. If you get a bad one you will become a philosopher, and that is good for any man."

Adopting the marketing concept may be a bit like getting married. It will require a long-term commitment with many binding and limiting requirements. Make it work effectively and you will have a happy and prosperous business. If you cannot structure the marketing concept so that it succeeds, you can always become a philosopher.

The academic disciplines of economics, sociology, and psychology view marketing through their own special windows to the world. The economist sees marketing as a minor subset of that field, concerned only with the movement of goods from the company to the consumer. The sociologist sees marketing as the source of manipulation of the consuming public. The psychologist's concern is how we motivate people to do our bidding.

It is only human to view any act through the special focus of our own experience and training. Thus the production person sees the company as having manufacturing at its core. The accounting people see the company through the filter of the balance sheet, and the finance person sees it through the cash-flow and profit-margin considerations. The legal department views the enterprise from the aspect of liability. Then there are the management information people, who believe that the right computer hardware operating on the proper software will focus the company properly.

Marketing is the only one of the business functions, with the possible exception of human resources, that continues to be everyone's province; indeed, it is sometimes staffed by professionals from other fields. People who have risen from other specialties, such as the technical side, legal, finance, or production, have little hesitancy in making critical marketing decisions in their companies. Lack of the critical insights that stem from experience and training in the methodology of the marketing function does not deter some people from involvement in critical marketing decisions.

This flows from a single root cause, we believe: the "everyman" approach to decisions. I am just like the customer; therefore I am everyman. I am a consumer; therefore I know what will stir or attract other consumers.

Unlike the case in most technical fields, marketing strategy is stated in terms understandable to all. This fact may lure lay people into an area where they are not necessarily suited to decision making. We also guess that marketing decisions are fun and challenging, and therefore it is interesting for nonprofessionals to wander through the marketing fields dabbling in decision making.

It is an important premise of this book that there is a comprehensible and realistic concept of marketing that is essential for effective management of any business enterprise. This premise sees marketing as not merely a basketful of specialties such as market research, advertising, selling, etc., but as an integrated function with its own evolving theory, a distinct methodology, and results-oriented practices.

This argues for the need to protect the marketing function and its qualified practitioners from the carping and meddling of neophytes, quacks, and lay people who lack the qualifications for intelligent decision making. It is true that marketing must constantly solicit input from every function of the business, but the know-nothing attitude that "My opinion is as good as yours" has no place in modern business decision making.

Even so, it is in everyone's interest for all executives, from every branch and function of an enterprise, to have marketing savvy. That sentiment led to the writing of this book.

We will try to clear up the confusion that surrounds the unique and peculiar relationship of the marketing function to the overall business. This is important because the marketing relationship differs in both nature and degree from that enjoyed by other functions. This relationship is not, as some have said, a functional grab for power and undue influence. It is an obligation rooted in the responsibility of the marketing organization to know, interpret, and influence the marketplace.

If the marketing manager is obligated to meet business goals for market share, growth, and an appropriate contribution to profitability, it is essential that marketing have major input and influence over product determination, pricing, and production scheduling to meet the sales requirements set for the company.

Consider the following statement:

> The purpose of marketing is to direct all aspects and functions of the company to the needs and standards of the marketplace and to direct all marketing activities to the objectives of the business enterprise.

To see how this statement is peculiar and unique to the marketing function, try substituting for *marketing* the names of functions, e.g., engineering, research and development, manufacturing, or finance. Such a substitution appears ridiculous, doesn't it? We believe this test best demonstrates marketing's unique relationship to the overall business.

The director of marketing of a Fortune 100 company puts it this way: "I see my job as, in part, [being] the customer advocate within this organization. I filter and communicate to the rest of the organization the comments and reactions that my staff and I constantly hear from the marketplace.

"My people, from the sales reps to the ad group and customer service, all know their responsibility for feeding back through me to the rest of the organization. We are the receptors in this vital communication process."

As we seek to implement and apply the marketing philosophy to the business, we must answer the following basic questions:

What is a business enterprise?
What is *our* business?
What is the vision for our business?
What is the image of our business?
What is the appropriate orientation for our business?

How will we get the marketing orientation implemented
throughout the business?
What commitments must we make in the marketplace?

Remember at all costs that as we move through the answers to these questions the operative word today in the business world is *change*. The one thing we can count on as an ongoing and dependable concept is change.

We need to implement the marketing concept in our business because marketing is uniquely qualified to:

Recognize change
Define change
Interpret change
Cope with change

If not the marketing function, then who?

Do we still need to pursue a definition of marketing? We
have said what it does; must we still define what it is? As with
knowing art when we see it, we believe that we best know marketing when we see it in action, not in a definition.

Old Wine in New Bottles?

Relationship marketing: knowing what your customers buy
from you, what their size is, what their growth goals are.

Database marketing: direct-mail marketing using com-
puter-manipulated data to target customers.

Blitzkrieg marketing: wide-range, broadcast, mass-media
marketing.

Affinity marketing: being open and receptive to the needs
of the customer; a merging of your culture and your customer's; partnering with your customers.

4

Determining the Nature of the Business

Marketing has much to offer the business person who attempts to determine the nature of the business entity. Marketing offers tools and a methodology to understand and position the business better. It can be summarized in these five steps:

1. Taking an inventory of the business, its strengths, and its weaknesses
2. Understanding the marketplace or arena in which the business functions
3. Developing a vision for the business
4. Establishing an image for the business
5. Defining the business charter

A Business Inventory

In every business, we periodically and methodically count the stock in the warehouse, the tools and equipment with which the business functions, and its current assets and liabilities. This is known universally as an inventory, a means of determining a company's stage of growth and development, status, progress, and rate of change.

Here, though, we are assessing the business in terms of the marketing concept. This takes our assessment into three areas:

Harold Evans, president of his own sports marketing company, says: "Marketing a product or service in the decade of the nineties requires a reorientation of outlook for many companies.

"There is such a clutter of offerings and events in the marketplace that we have to revisit the venerable concept of the *unique selling proposition*. When an event is ready to go to market, we must make certain that there is a singular aspect to the promotion. The term *unique* has become a cliché, I'm afraid, but it is still mandatory that to climb up out of that clutter, our event

- Have distinctiveness,
- Be memorable, and
- Be targeted to a specific audience.

"And we must have found a way to communicate all of this to its market.

"We find this a great test for our marketing planning. If we have failed on any one of these counts, we will likely have a failed event."

---

1. The market segments served—here we determine which segments of the market will be important in the future
2. The products and services offered—here we determine which of our offerings have the best odds for future payoff
3. The strengths and weaknesses of the company in each market—here we measure present and future prospects as we envision them

In doing this kind of inventory, we are preparing for the strategic planning process presented in Part Three. We will utilize it again in the market appraisal proposed in Part Five.

The Marketplace

This is the business arena—the marketplace—where the action for a company truly is. This is where customers, the distribution mix, competitors, and the general business environment all interact to create the arena of activity and excitement that we call the marketplace.

Be certain you realize that most companies are in more than one arena or marketplace. Realize that they are constantly changing as well. The dynamics of a marketplace are subject to all of the forces that change can exert on all three of the elements we have mentioned above.

In Chapter 11 we discuss the systems and tools of intelligence that can be used for this purpose.

A Vision for the Business

What business are we really in? This is a more subtle question than it initially appears to be. The answer includes such considerations as the present status of the business in each marketplace as it is factored into the future, near- and long-term.

How, when, and where do we expect change to occur? What is our forecast for each market segment in which we have a stake? Where do we want to be in each segment? What are the scale, the direction, the pace, the goals, and the strategy required to get us there?

These are the vision questions that the marketing concept asks the marketing manager to answer in a practical, realistic, and timely manner.

Let's take a look at the shoe business as an example. Assume that there are three distinct segments to be evaluated. Is it the vision of the company to appeal to the prestige and vanity of affluent, style-conscious, high-fashion customers? Or will it appeal to the sense of thrift, modesty, and the functional needs of the mass market? Or will it be to the latest fads and whims of the trendy?

If the answer is yes to all three questions, we must recognize that each is a quite different business. A different vision must be prepared for each. These are actually separate businesses and each must be treated uniquely.

A New York retail jeweler demonstrates clear and consistent vision with a store operated on Madison Avenue. Every aspect of the operation speaks to the vision management has for the business. The unusual and attractive merchandise, the merchandising style used to present it, the nature and essence of the promotions used, and the personal service offered to the clientele all reflect the vision of the business. The catalog the company mails to its customer list carries the same appeal and reflects the same values. Pricing, ambience, and presentation are similarly consistent.

As a result, the store attracts customers who relate to and identify with management's vision. They have a clear impression of the store because management has defined its vision, and every aspect of the business speaks to that vision.

Having made a choice of vision for the company, management must raise and answer the following questions:

1. Is the vision clearly stated and understood?
2. Is the style of management in character with it?
3. Is the vision understood and reflected by all of the employees?
4. Are the products, pricing policies, strategies, and all activities of the company supporting and implementing this vision?
5. Are there practices anywhere in the operation that are inconsistent with the vision as stated?
6. Are all of the key people constantly monitoring the implementation of the vision and applying adjustments and correctives when necessary?
7. Are all communications to the customer, such as advertising and in-store promotions, synchronized to implement the vision?

An important point on this subject of the company's mission: Remember, the business must be viewed in longer-range terms than just the present. Seeing its future means anticipating the need for change and the means to adapt and to achieve it.

Adaptation is as mandatory in the commercial world as it is in the biological environment. Failure or inability to adapt to change can doom a business as fatally as it does any living organism. The theories of social Darwinism apply equally to business. Adapt to changes in the environment, or die. Only the fit will survive.

The methods and tools used in strategic planning presented in Part Three and those of marketing appraisal presented in Part Five will be helpful in developing a vision for the business and evaluating its impact.

An Image of the Business

The term *image* has almost been reduced to a cliché, almost destroyed by overuse and misuse. However, it still has much utility when properly applied.

Marketing people have a legitimate assignment to conceive, develop, and maintain an integrated, consistent image for the company. The image must be centered on providing for customer needs and wants. At the same time, this image must reflect back into the company itself and to its employees that their every action and statement must reinforce the image that is the outward manifestation of the company.

Every function of the company, visible to the outside world or not, communicates the company image. This communica-

---

Wal-Mart has made enormous inroads into small-town America at the expense of the Main Street merchant by providing all of the close and personal service of the small store combined with the enormous inventory and low pricing that massive buying quantities permit.

Every customer is greeted upon entering the store. He or she is directed to the area of interest. Help is available to answer questions and provide support.

Such service is just not found in other large retail operations. In most of them, it is impossible even to identify store employees, much less find a salesperson. Every Wal-Mart employee wears distinctive dress and a name tag. In every aspect of the store, the customer's needs are the central focus.

---

tion is by no means limited to the visibility that advertising and promotion attain.

Such organizations as Wal-Mart and Nordstrom carefully craft their image, first cultivating it with their own people and then communicating it to the customer. It is rare that such companies fail to live up to their image with their clientele.

Some businesses present an utterly confused image, both inside and outside the company. This is a costly failure of leadership. No amount of expensive puffery will compensate for the lack of either a consistent image program or diligence in promoting it. It is important to note that a carefully crafted image can be seriously damaged by a single instance of inappropriate implementation.

Market studies demonstrate again and again that customers return to a particular product, store, or manufacturer even in the face of elaborate and expensive blandishments by competitors. Why? Because of the satisfaction received—and because of the reliability and integrity of the image projected.

Retailers have been able to establish private store brands with their customers that are based on the image projected by the store in the face of all of the advertising and lures of well-established brands. This is the rub-off from the image projected by the store.

Projection of an accepted image and its acceptance by the

Nordstrom, the expanding department-store chain, has trained its salespeople to respond to a customer's inquiry with a storewide attitude and a customer-centered focus. If the customer is interested in a turtleneck shirt, the salesperson will travel to several departments to collect merchandise for the customer and show samples of each department's offerings. Compare this with the more common attitude of: "Try one of the other departments in the store if my merchandise is not to your liking." Or worse: "That's all we have, sorry."

The benefits to the store's image are apparent. The likelihood of ultimately satisfying and selling the customer and, most importantly, of bringing that customer back into the store on a subsequent buying trip is greatly improved.

---

public represents value worth millions to a store. Advertising cannot buy this kind of recognition. It represents valuable free publicity for the store or the manufacturer.

A brand name is really the result of a successful projection of an image to the public. The fact that some product names have achieved generic status, describing the whole class of similar products, is testimony to the impact of that image. Names like Jell-O, Kleenex, Xerox, Walkman, and other such brand names are accepted as the standard by which all others are judged by the public.

The Business Charter

In a company where there is substantial complexity in product lines, markets, or the sales and distribution channels employed, a charter statement must be stated. This is also true of a company where there are several interdependent or related businesses. A charter has the benefit of maintaining clarity and purpose in the relationships among the various businesses.

The charter defines and describes each element of the company, to help accomplish orderly changes in the scope and relationships of organizational elements. It is also useful for avoiding or resolving internal conflicts among the lines of business.

A charter for each business unit would include:

- A statement of the nature and intent of the unit and of the vision proposed for it
- An outline of the broad, continuing objectives and strategies for the unit and for each of its major segments
- A delineation of the scope of the business unit, with each market segment defined in terms of activities, products, and markets
- A definition of important continuing relationships, both internal and external
- A commitment to exploration and development in the areas of products, services, and distribution beyond the present scope of the unit

There is a tendency to view units of a company only in terms of products and facilities, overlooking their markets and distribution dimensions. A charter program will help to overcome this problem.

An Illustration of a Charter Approach

In the home appliance business, an electric-range company may be in several businesses:

1. Ranges for the replacement home market, sold through retail distribution
2. Ranges for the construction market, sold through contractors
3. Ranges for the mobile home market, sold directly to manufacturers

Product characteristics may be substantially different for each of the three business segments. Management must recognize that three separate businesses are involved here.

A charter program can also facilitate the decision to enter a new business or to drop an existing one. Equally important is the provision for authorizing exploratory and development effort, thereby avoiding gaps in the growth program and avoiding duplication of activity among the business units.

This Is Our Business

The myriad present-day activities reflecting mergers, divestitures, technological changes and complexities, and the diversity of distribution options make it increasingly important that management be able to say: *"This* is our business."

5

Selecting the Orientation of Your Business

One of the most fundamental decisions for management in any business is to determine its basic orientation. Where the orientation is inappropriate, ill defined, or confused, the organization lacks common purpose. Functional conflicts are accentuated, and turmoil is sure to result. Teamwork suffers, inefficiency prevails, and economic performance is severely handicapped.

The process of selecting an orientation requires considerable analysis and careful choices that suit the external conditions and limitations of the operation.

We have selected five orientations commonly seen in business: production, sales, technology, finance, and marketing.

The following descriptions are from a marketing viewpoint and reflect that bias.

Production Orientation

This is the traditional orientation of a manufacturing business. Some principal characteristics are that:

- The focus and emphasis are on the factory and the making of products
- Limited attention is given to market research and product planning

- Cost-reduction efforts may sacrifice product quality and performance, and possibly customer service
- There is a tendency to base pricing on cost alone, with value and competitive considerations downplayed
- The role of the sales force is to sell what the factory makes
- If customers express dissatisfaction, the sales people are directed to find new ones

Businesses serving industrial and commercial markets with mass-produced products are the most likely adherents to this orientation. There is an interesting counterpart in wholesaling and retailing enterprises: a "procurement" orientation, with emphasis on selection of merchandise but without adequate attention to customer desires and marketplace influences.

Sales Orientation

As we shall see, there are fundamental differences here between a sales and a marketing orientation. The characteristics of a sales orientation are that:

- The focus is on volume, not on profit
- The customer should be given what is wanted, regardless of the cost to the business
- There may be weak linkage between true customers' wants and needs and the product planning required to fulfill them
- Pricing, credit, and service policies may be loosely stated and adhered to
- Production schedules may be heavily influenced by optimistic sales estimates
- Communications from the market to engineering and manufacturing are commonly inadequate

In some respects, a sales orientation is the converse of a production orientation. Where a sales orientation occurs, the

Kenneth Olsen, retiring president of giant computer manufacturer Digital Equipment Corporation, explained to his employees the failures that led to his removal. He said that he was never able to make necessary changes in the product line quickly enough because the managers who ran engineering units failed to cooperate with the managers who marketed products.

The power struggle between these groups resulted in DEC's continuing to build too many products that it could not sell. As an example, the marketing people surveying the customer base reported back that just two distinct types of computers were needed. Marketing communicated this to engineering—which still came back with fifteen new products because engineering said it had the capacity to design and produce them.

sales organization tends to dominate the organization. This is common in businesses where volume is considered to have strong leverage on profits.

Many retail and wholesale businesses continue to emphasize a sales orientation even after competitive conditions have called for a change of focus.

Technology Orientation

This is most commonly found in highly technical enterprises. It may also be maintained in businesses which have their roots in technological change or development. Some of the predominant features are that:

- The emphasis is on research and engineering per se, with inadequate recognition of other economic considerations
- Market criteria to guide the research and development function are inadequate
- There is little planning influence from marketing
- The tendency is to over-engineer products beyond what the customer needs or is willing to pay for

- Product, development, and facility decisions between engineering and manufacturing are made without the participation of the marketing people

This orientation prevails in many industrial and utility businesses, and in the aerospace and defense fields, where technology requirements are high. The basis of this orientation is the belief that only engineers and scientists are competent to understand the business and make the key decisions.

Finance Orientation

In many companies, this orientation has become almost absolute in its power and influence over other functions. Many feel that this influence has not always been a positive one, as it affects management decisions. These are some of the reasons:

- The emphasis tends to be on short-range profit at the expense of growth and longer-range profit
- Budgeting and forecasting frequently preempt or dominate business planning
- Efficiency may overpower effectiveness as a management criterion for action
- Decisions on pricing, costs, credit, service, design, and engineering may be based on misguided economizing and lack of a sense of the marketplace
- The business focus is not on the customer and the market but on internal considerations and "the numbers"

In his book *The Reckoning*, David Halberstam puts much of the blame for the U.S. loss of market share in the automobile business on the growing influence of finance-oriented managers, at the expense of design and engineering specialists.[1] You may add to this the lack of influence on the part of marketing people as well.

The accounting and finance systems, deeply rooted in the

[1]David Halberstam, *The Reckoning* (New York: William Morrow, 1986).

legal and tax requirements of the business and in short-term financial results, do not always serve the business well. Their influence on sales and expense allocations, marketing decisions, and production commitments has at times insulated management from the needs of the marketplace and the activities of competitors.

Marketing Orientation

Much lip service is paid to this orientation, but there is still widespread failure to implement this approach fully and knowledgeably. Some of its basic features are:

- A focus on the marketplace and its elements (customers, competition, and distribution)
- An intelligence system that constantly and consistently monitors the marketplace
- A recognition that change in the business arena is inevitable but manageable
- A commitment to strategic business and marketing planning coupled with creative product planning

---

Gerald C. Rittenberg, executive vice president of Amscan, a major manufacturer and marketer in the party goods and gift field, directs his product managers to spend at least one day every week out in the marketplace visiting retailers and watching customers' buying patterns.

"This helps them to determine the *whys* and *hows* of the business," Charles says. "Now they know why a particular product (ours or a competitor's) sells; why it doesn't; how our first-level customer, the retailer, views product; and, most importantly, how our second-line customer, the consumer, views the products we and our competitors offer.

"You cannot be a marketing manager in this company and simply operate inside our office building. It is happening out there."

Source: Interview with author.

- An emphasis on profit, not just volume, with growth as an additional factor

Do not confuse customer focus with marketing orientation. While marketing considers the customer's needs, it is broad enough to include an awareness of the influences of competition and distribution. This breadth maintains a balance between external market considerations and the internal requirements of the business itself.

A Balanced View of the Business

Many managers have made the mistake of interpreting the marketing concept as a complete shift from a focus on the company's resources to a naïve focus on the customer's needs and wants. They assume that they have only to turn their attention to the marketplace and all will be well with the business. Would that life in business were so simple.

The marketing concept and a market orientation demand a more balanced view of the business (see Figure 1). This requires study, analysis, and judicious decision making. We may start sizing up the business *either* with customer needs, wants, and whims, or with the company's resources.

Let's take a new product or technology as an example. If we have an adequate grasp of and information about the marketplace, we can equally well start not with the customer but with the company's own resources and ability to manufacture or produce a new product utilizing the new technology.

Regardless of where the process starts, we must strive for balance between the needs of the customer and the ability of the business to serve them. This process recognizes that it is possible to create or develop demand. It also recognizes that company resources can be modified, or even superseded, as the enterprise adjusts to market opportunities.

This is all done in light of the competitive considerations that prevail in the marketplace. The reaction of competitors to the moves you make and your reactions to their moves are vital

Figure 1.   A balanced view of the business.

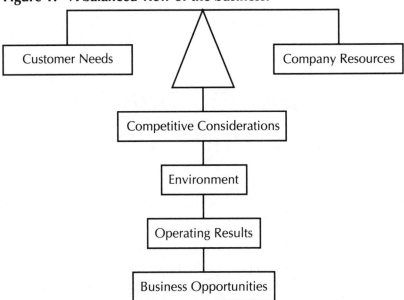

to the choice of opportunities and strategies you select for your company.

Similarly, changes in the business environment in which your company operates will have a vital effect on your decisions. Social, economic, political, and physical factors in the environment must be taken into account.

Not the least of these considerations is the ultimate effect on the operating results of the organization. Employment, equipment and facility needs, and investment requirements are critical questions to be answered.

Thus we interrelate customer needs and company resources to make an orderly and rational selection of business opportunities.

6

Implementing the Marketing Concept

The decision to adopt the marketing concept calls for major commitments. This concept can have substantial impact on every business function and procedure. It probably requires changes in organization and usually demands new approaches to planning.

There may be some surprises experienced in the process. It may uncover performance weaknesses and call for changes in policy and practices. Long-established attitudes may have to be changed. Expect objections, obstacles, resistance, and the need to overcome deeply rooted habits.

Frequently, difficult and painful restaffing programs are necessary before any real progress can be made in implementing the marketing concept.

The Need for Preplanning

Preplanning is necessary to develop an orderly program of communication for the planned installation of the marketing concept. Such actions during the initial phases will help to smooth the way for implementation.

Several studies, by business-school professors and their graduate students, of implementation of the marketing concept disclose some helpful patterns. It is useful to know that a substantial majority of large and medium-size companies have adopted the marketing concept. However, many have not achieved desired levels of marketing orientation.

This lack of progress in moving to a sophisticated implementation stage is understandable when you consider what is necessary for successful implementation:

- A complete understanding of the marketing concept
- Strong top-level sponsorship and commitment
- Professional leadership in marketing
- Comprehensive planning prior to adoption and implementation of the marketing concept

Sponsorship

It is essential to have sponsorship and support at the highest levels of the organization in order to initiate, adopt, and implement this new way of business life. These executives must:

- Thoroughly understand the nature of the commitments required
- Recognize the impact this move will have on their own attitudes and policy decisions
- Be prepared to deal with the resistance to be met
- Accept leadership responsibility to facilitate acceptance and implementation of this new philosophy
- Acknowledge the need to make their own actions and decisions harmonize with the marketing concept
- Mandate functional integration and teamwork that are compatible with a marketing orientation

The Marketing Manager

Of almost equal importance to the commitment of top executives is the selection of the right marketing manager to spearhead the implementation program. This person must be granted authority and responsibility commensurate with the importance of the task to be accomplished.

This role must be filled by a professional who commands the respect of peers in the organization and in professional marketing circles as well.

Relationships With the Other Functions

The marketing manager and key associates will find it necessary to build new relationships with the other functions of the business. The marketing team will utilize knowledge gained from the commercial-intelligence and product-planning activities they engage in.

With respect to research and development and engineering, the marketing team is in a position to:

- Provide marketplace guidance to improve existing products
- Facilitate development of new offerings

In working with production, marketers can:

- Facilitate production scheduling through improved communication about sales requirements
- Help improve quality control through monitoring and feedback from product service
- Provide a sound basis for facility and personnel planning through more accurate forecasting

With the financial organization, the marketing team can:

- Bring together product planners and cost accountants to deal with product costs and pricing
- Bring together distribution and cost accountants to better plan and allocate distribution costs
- Help to perform better all of the budgeting and forecasting activities

Gerard B. Halpin, executive vice president of Carswell, a major purveyor of print and electronic legal reference material to the Canadian market, says: "We have now succeeded in closely linking all the functions in our company so that we all hear the same drumbeat and we are all marching to it.

"Our design, product development, manufacturing, marketing, and sales groups share the final vision of the product at the same time and in the same dimensions. We are now seeing a faster development cycle with considerably less revision needed. And, most important to me, all the functions have taken ownership of the idea and are nurturing it as if it were their own."

Source: Interview with author.

The Marketing Orientation

A true marketing orientation keeps all eyes focused on the marketplace to continuously evaluate customers, competition, and the business environment. It means knowing what customers want, what they consider to be of value, and what they will pay. It means managing the business to fulfill these expectations so that the customer is satisfied, communicates this to other consumers, and, above all, comes back to buy again.

With such a fundamental change in the business philosophy, the marketing concept must be explained clearly to the whole organization.

The teamwork required to make all of this happen must be discussed with appropriate personnel from all functions. It will be accepted and implemented if it is presented in terms of realizable benefits to each of the functions and to overall business performance.

Communication of the Concept

For successful implementation, it is necessary to have a program aimed at gaining understanding of the marketing concept, earning acceptance of it, and promoting actions in support of the concept from all concerned. Elements of this communications program include:

- A statement of the concept, reasons for its adoption, and an outline of implementation plans
- Convening meetings featuring open discussion among all of the affected functions, to explain, clarify, and promote the concept
- Periodic reminders in publications and in meetings so as to report progress, deal with obstacles and objections, and continue to promote the program

Marketing Policies

Adoption of the marketing concept calls for a review of marketing policies and, when necessary, development of modifications. Subjects for review are:

- Product line—rules and procedures for adding new products, modifying existing ones, and dropping old ones
- Pricing—stating a pricing policy, delegating authority for pricing, and creating procedures for price changes
- Distribution—guidelines for establishing distributors, dealers, and agents, for dealing with them on a continuing basis, and for ending such arrangements
- Product service—stating the philosophy of service and support after the sale, including warranties, pricing, and establishment of service agencies
- Trademarks and brands—a procedure for authorizing the use of trademarks and brand names, private branding, secondary names, and labeling

These are only a few examples of policy subjects. Each business develops its own list of subjects.

We suggest the following principles for operation of a policy system:

- Formally publish policy statements (unwritten policies are subject to varied interpretations)
- All members of the organization affected should be given the opportunity to review and make suggestions or raise objections
- Formal policy statements should be restricted to major subjects (procedural matters can be handled through other means of communications)
- Consider policy a formal law of an organization (policy statements must not be issued unless they can and will be honored by all)

Implementation

The marketing staff will need to meet periodically to evaluate progress. Checklists of topics and questions should be created, to consider such items as:

1. The marketplace
   - Do we regularly and systematically analyze our markets?
   - Do we understand and use market segmentation?
   - Do we have adequate information and intelligence to manage effectively?
   - Are we satisfied with our communications to and from our customers?
2. Products and services
   - Are we taking a creative approach to product planning?
   - Do we have product leadership?
   - How do we rate in product quality, product performance, and overall value?
   - What services do we sell before, during, and after the sale?
   - Are our policies and practices competitive?
   - Will our customers agree with our answers?
3. Advertising and promotion
   - Are we addressing our messages to our customers, not to ourselves?

- Is our selection of media focused on important market segments?
- Do our aids to our distributors and dealers effectively assist them in carrying out their tasks?
- Are our advertising and our agency market-focused, not just client-focused?
- Do we evaluate our promotions by their impact on customers?

4. Sales and distribution
   - Are our customers being served where and how they wish?
   - Does the distribution chain share our aims and values?
   - Are all of the elements in the chain marketing-oriented?

5. Service to customers
   - Do we know what services our customers want and expect?
   - What will they pay for such services?
   - Are we aligned with, or ahead of, competition in this area?
   - Do we know our customers' expectations as to delivery, quality, and pricing?
   - Are we satisfying our customer's expectations?

The marketing performance checklist in Part Five will also be useful in formulating questions. Of course, all such questions must be adapted to your business.

Next in order is formulation of a teamwork program, to be undertaken with each of the functions in the business.

In taking these steps, you prepare an implementation program for your business.

Part Two
A Market-Oriented Organization

7

The Focus
of the Business

A business can take one of two directions in its focus: an internal or an external outlook. The internal focus serves the company's own purposes, its convenience, its employees' needs, its stockholders' and owners' interests. There is certainly nothing wrong with this approach to the business in and of itself.

The alternative focus comprises the marketplace, the customers' needs and the status of the competition. We face this dichotomy just as soon as we attempt to install and implement the marketing concept.

The responsibility lies with the marketing function to lead the building of a marketing-oriented organization. Marketing must see to it that the overall business structure and its components are designed, oriented, and staffed to serve our customers effectively. Marketing people must facilitate this outlook among all of the other functions of the company as well. Teamwork is the operative word here. The customer is the focus for the *entire* organization.

The concept of the efficient and productive profit center continues in a marketing-oriented organization, but traditional forms of organization and traditional organizational values and systems need review and possibly change.

Let's take an example in a department store, where menswear traditionally has had the following departments:

Shirts
Sweaters

Neckwear
Suits and coats
Haberdashery
Shoes
Sportswear

If each of these departments retains its traditional buying habits for the convenience of managers and employees, what is missing? The entire marketing orientation, with its focus on the *customers*, their buying habits and needs, and the state and outlook of the competition.

Something else may well be missing: teamwork and coordination among all of the other functions in the store, to make certain that the customer remains at the center of the universe of the entire store.

Barney's, the New York men's store now expanding into other major cities, and Louis, the highly regarded Boston men's outfitter, have developed this strategy to a fine art. The salesperson assigned to a customer stays with that person through the entire stay. The salespeople are not departmentalized but are instead focused on customer needs. That way, the store maximizes its sales opportunities, and the customer receives a high level of personal attention every step of the way.

Organizing Principles

As we contemplate the process of designing an organizational form to accomplish our goal of a marketing-oriented company, certain standards and values must be observed:

- Look ahead, not just backwards at what has been
- Responsibility and authority must be equal within a function
- Accountability must be installed at every level
- Staffing must be adequate to the new task and not mired in the traditions of the past
- Clarify each function's communications needs and channels with every other department

- Delineate which services will be performed internally and which by outside providers
- Ascertain that every function understands its relationship with and responsibility to every other function

In other words, if it's not "broke," maybe it should be.

Setting the Style

Usually, organizations are better at dealing with structure than with style, because they are more familiar with that approach. This is perfectly understandable, because it is easier to sit at a desk and create organization/function charts, with their two-dimensional boxes and solid and dotted lines, than to create and nurture a *style* of doing business.

The task here is very different and many times more challenging. To install the marketing concept in a traditional organization requires an understanding and appreciation of the range of styles available.

Formal vs. Informal

Both styles exist, to an extent, in every organization. The formal encompasses the specific chains of command and communications channels that management has mandated. The informal aspect is the network of relationships, influences, and communications that have evolved among the people in the organization.

We do not propose to disband the formal aspects of the organization. But a determination has to be made as to recognizing and utilizing the power of the informal organization in installing the marketing concept.[1]

Centralized vs. Decentralized

Here we are dealing with delegated and withheld authority. The centralized organization is typically functional. The decen-

[1]See Chester I. Barnard, *The Functions of the Executive* (Cambridge, Mass.: Harvard University Press, 1968), for a thoughtful exposition of the respective roles of formal and informal organizations.

tralized company usually features a structure emphasizing profit centers and product lines or services. Under either organizational structure, however, management can still decide to take a highly centralized or decentralized approach to the decision process, policy making, controls, and the degree and depth of participation in decision making. These approaches may be free and permissive, or highly limiting.

Autocratic vs. Democratic

The autocratic approach parallels that of the traditional military or dictatorial governmental style, tending to be dogmatic, critical, and closely controlled. The democratic style permits, encourages, and utilizes broad participation in decisions and open communication channels.

Mechanistic vs. Organic

The mechanistic organization employs many specialized positions with precise and carefully defined tasks. It is hierarchical, and in stable business conditions it can be used effectively. The organic structure is more dependent on individuals with highly specialized capabilities that are contributed to the common tasks. Relationships develop informally, based on mutual respect and the communicative abilities of the participants. The roles adjust to conditions, which makes the organic approach more effective when there are extensive and frequent changes in market conditions and technology.

Vertical vs. Horizontal

The vertical organization favors more structural levels, while the horizontal organization employs broader scope at each structural level. The vertical requires more managers and supervisors, with complicated communication and decision making. The horizontal employs wider managerial spans, with some loss of control and direction. The task here is to arrive at whatever balance between the horizontal and vertical approaches best suits the needs of the specific business.

Effective vs. Efficient

These two approaches raise an important distinction. A style that emphasizes the effective approach focuses on performance and results as measured in profit and growth. By contrast, a style that emphasizes efficiency stresses cost control and cost reduction. The latter frequently saves pennies but loses dollars by failing to eliminate some positions and activities, instead trying to make them more efficient and economical. Once again, we are looking for balance.

Carrot vs. Club

The carrot style features encouragement, incentives, rewards, and praise to motivate people to higher performance. The club style employs criticism, firm appraisals, tight controls, and close supervision. Choose a style, and use it consistently. Erratic shifts, from whims or the emotions of a manager, can cause confusion and morale problems.

Specialist vs. Generalist

We must decide whether to emphasize specialized or generalized positions. An example is a shift from product-line sales people to an account focus. Often such moves are made as a business grows in size or complexity in its number of lines, diversity of markets, and forms of distribution.

Work vs. People

A work-focused style employs detailed work planning by managers. It emphasizes specification of the methods to be used, and it requires close supervision. The people-focused style emphasizes selection of the right people, with the employees expected to do their own work planning, to select appropriate work methods, and to appraise their performance themselves.

Individual vs. Group

In the first instance, a person has precisely designated tasks to perform. In the second, there will be teams, committees, task forces, and other forms of group assignments. Care must be taken to find the right balance between the two approaches. Where interfunctional responsibilities call for complex decisions, as in product planning, the group approach is usually more desirable.

Integrated vs. Coordinated

The integrated approach assumes overall business planning with common objectives and strategies. It uses staff meetings and other such means of communication to achieve teamwork. The coordinated approach provides specialized staff positions, such as advisory specialists, functional supervisors, troubleshooters, and appraisers, to pull various activities together.

Calm vs. Conflict

The calm approach assumes that people perform best where there is little excitement, pressure, or confusion. Under the conflict style, it is assumed excitement, pressure, and controlled confusion contribute to performance. The choice here depends on the personality and character of both leaders and employees. Organizations seem to vary. Some appear to be most productive under a calm style, while others appear to thrive on conflict.

Climate vs. System

As used here, *climate* relates to what employees like and want in the environment in which they work. Management anticipates and makes an effort to suit these demands. Where the systems approach is emphasized, there is an organizational approach in which work flow, relationships, and expectations are planned and function in an orderly, sequential, and mechanical fashion.

Selecting a Style

Observation of successful management styles provides the following guidelines:

- The style selected should be appropriate to the situation; it must fit the marketplace, the industry, and the competitive arena.
- The style of the marketing organization needs to be in harmony with that of the overall business.
- The style should be compatible with the vision and image of the business.
- The style should be compatible with the character and the personality of the marketing manager.
- Consistency of style is essential to avoid confusion and conflict.

The temptation is great to follow each new fad or fashion. Such pressure must be resisted. You must recognize that appropriateness and consistency are the guidelines, and that whimsical, trendy change can be upsetting and costly.

Contrasts in Style

Let's look at the styles of two actual marketing managers who work in the same organization.

Chet generally ignores his organization's formal structure. He often speaks on personnel development and runs lots of courses for his people. He puts personnel development at the top of his objectives list. He sponsors frequent social affairs for his associates and their spouses. He talks all the time about performance appraisals.

Charlene respects organizational channels. Her personnel development program involves giving interesting and challenging work assignments. She is always available to her subordinates. She acts as coach and consultant on their work whenever they ask. She makes higher-level contacts available to them. She makes tough and fair performance appraisals regularly.

Chet is feared, generally disliked, and rarely supported by his people. His contribution to the development of strong, competent people is meager.

Charlene is respected and liked, and she has the support

of the entire organization. She has earned a reputation for developing outstanding people who get regular promotions.

The structure is the same, the product lines identical, the marketplaces comparable. But the differences are profound. It is clearly a matter of style, of course. The human factor in management matters greatly, and marketing is no exception to this rule.

8

Marketing Relationships

The Scope of Marketing

We need to clarify for ourselves and for the entire business organization the scope and reach of the marketing function.

This is how one major company has stated marketing's scope in terms of its purpose and responsibility to the business.

1. To formulate and recommend to top management long- and short-range marketing plans for the business in terms of products, customers, sales channels, and prices
2. To formulate, execute, and measure marketing programs to achieve these plans, and to integrate the performance of these activities with other functions of the business

Definition of the scope of marketing in a specific company is an essential step. As changes in management or structure take place within an organization, it is vital for all concerned to have a clear and concise statement of the scope of marketing. This eliminates confusion and possible conflict and makes clear what is to be provided by the marketing organization.

Marketing Functions

To avoid misunderstanding, we need to be sure that all concerned do not confuse functions with structure. Functions are the work to be done. The structure is the arrangement and assignment of those functions into the organizational makeup.

Marketing activities break down into several distinct areas. Here is one of the more common classifications:

• *Marketing research.* This includes data, facts, and figures for planning and daily operations, as regards customers, markets, competitors, and the general environment. It embraces research in all aspects of marketing. Some of this effort is on a project basis; other work is done continuously.

• *Product planning.* This includes new products, modifications, eliminations, pricing policy and formulation, industrial design, packaging, branding, and other product-related activities.

• *Advertising and sales promotion.* This includes all forms of marketing communication, in all media. It embraces market development, preselling and sales, and product information provided to buyers. Also included are plans for point-of-purchase merchandising.

• *Sales and distribution.* This includes sales planning and administration, selling (directly to the customer and through the distribution channels), sales training, and customer relations.

• *Product service.* This includes identifying and satisfying customer expectations for service after the sale is made, including warranties, replacements, handling complaints, and other aspects of customer service.

• *Marketing administration.* This includes sales forecasting, sales and marketing budgets, production scheduling to meet sales and market requirements, physical distribution, order service and fulfillment, and any other aspects of business management for the marketing function.

• *Marketing personnel.* This includes personnel forecasting and planning, recruiting, placement, development and training, compensation, and performance appraisal.

This is a standard functional classification for marketing. There are alternative structures of the functions. One that some prefer is:

• *Marketing information.* Operation of the commercial intelligence system; economic, industry and sales forecasting; and marketing research.

• *Marketing planning.* Participation in overall business planning; development of overall marketing plans; and product planning, including new products, modifications and eliminations, pricing, product design, and packaging.

• *Marketing communications.* Advertising, merchandising and sales promotion; market development programs; sales development programs; and publishing services for the company.

• *Sales and distribution.* Sales planning; distribution planning; sales and distribution analysis, administration and control; selling and customer relations; proposals and quotations; and sales training.

• *Marketing administration support.* Support-system planning, including physical distribution; sales budgeting; marketing records and statistics; marketing-expense budgets; marketing-office management; production scheduling to meet sales requirements; product inventory control; operation of the physical distribution system, including warehousing, transportation, and delivery; order and fulfillment service; and product service.

• *Marketing personnel.* Manpower planning; recruiting, selection and placement; sales development and training; compensation and performance appraisal; and personnel relations.

Since work requirements and accepted nomenclature vary from business to business, it is essential to select a functional classification appropriate to the specific enterprise. For example, banks and insurance companies, retail establishments, and transportation companies have activities unique to themselves and special terminology that must be considered in providing a functional classification for their purposes.

Formalizing Marketing Relationships

Special attention must be given to clarifying the formal and informal provisions for facilitating communications, decision making, and teamwork. It is essential to develop relationship analyses appropriate to the specific company and industry.

There are four major areas that require consideration:

1. Those involving teamwork within the entire company
2. Those between marketing and other functions
3. Those with external groups
4. Those within marketing

The following checklists are useful to demonstrate the kinds of activities that often call for clarification of a relationship.

Teamwork for the Overall Business

Many of the most important business activities call for participation and cooperation from all functions. The following require contributions from marketing:

- Business information systems
- Overall business planning
- Product planning
- Product performance—quality, service, and safety
- Pricing and value planning
- Production scheduling
- Physical distribution
- Cost reduction
- Operations research
- Performance measurement

We need to clarify the extent and nature of marketing's participation and contribution in each activity. Also, we need to designate the particular individual in marketing who has the responsibility for representing the function in this teamwork effort.

Relationships With Other Functions

Marketing has important shared responsibilities and teamwork obligations with each of the other business functions. These need to be analyzed from a marketing point of view and, in each case, reviewed with representatives of the other functions. Here are some of the major areas for consideration in a manufacturing business (adapt this list to other types of businesses):

Research and engineering

- Product planning
- Product quality and performance
- Product service
- Application engineering
- Development of quotations and requisitions

Manufacturing and production

- Production scheduling to meet sales requirements
- Inventory planning and control
- Product cost
- Quality control
- Product service

Accounting and finance

- Product costs
- Pricing
- Budgeting and forecasting
- Credit and collections

Human resources

- Compensation and incentive programs
- Training responsibilities
- Manpower planning

Legal

- Marketing policies
- Franchises
- Contracts
- Trade practices

In analyzing these relationships, you should seek to define marketing responsibilities and the authority basis with the other functions.

Relationships With External Groups

These relationships will vary according to the type of industry, the characteristics of the enterprise, and the overall philosophy and policies of incumbent management.

The following list suggests the external relationships that warrant analysis:

Customers

- Customer relations policies
- Contact responsibilities
- Trade relations
- Contracts
- Warranties

Distribution

- Dealers
- Distributors
- Agents
- Franchises
- Promotions
- Education
- Performance evaluation

Competitors

- Do's and don'ts for company personnel
- Permitted- and restricted-information exchange
- Commercial intelligence procedures

Service and material vendors

- Advertising agencies
- Marketing research

- Consultants
- Training suppliers

Government

- Monitoring legislation
- Agency activities
- Judicial rulings
- Influencing political and governmental policies and decisions

Associations

- Participation in trade and general business organizations

This relationships analysis should consider the nature and amount of work required of the marketing organization, the need for policy and procedure development, and the assignment of contact responsibility within the marketing staff.

Relationships Within Marketing

Since marketing includes a variety of functions, proper integration of effort requires special attention. The concern is to identify problems relating to communications, decision authority, and any roadblocks to teamwork.

Consider the following outlines of some common relationships to be explored:

- Linkage of market research and commercial intelligence to product planning
- Utilization of marketing research for planning and evaluating sales and distribution, advertising, sales promotion, and product service activities
- Formulation and implementation of pricing policies and practices with product planning and sales units
- Definition of responsibility for market segments, product lines, and distribution channels

- Integration of advertising and sales promotion with sales and distribution for optimum impact
- Integration of product service with product planning and field sales
- Interaction among sales forecasting, budgeting, and production scheduling
- Coordination of recruiting and training activities with other marketing units, particularly sales and product service

Marketing people should be encouraged to resolve relationship problems at the lowest possible level of the organization. Marketing management will occasionally need to intercede to require integration of effort among all the marketing people.

Product Planning Teams

At times, the complexity of the product-planning process calls for special organizational provisions. The use of product teams has proven very effective for this purpose. Principal considerations in establishing such teams are that:

- Teams should be used to integrate the contributions of all of the functions.
- Teams may work on a project basis or continuously, but provision should be made for continuity.
- Teams may be convened for adaptation of a new technology, redesigning a product line, or evaluating a new business opportunity.

Keep in mind the distinctions between product planning as an integrated activity of all of the relevant functions in the company and product planning and management as a purely marketing activity.

9

Structuring the Marketing Department

The process proposed here is equally useful for designing a wholly new marketing organization or for evaluating and overhauling an existing operation.

At this point, we must select an organizational structure for the marketing organization. Several criteria can be used to make this decision. Here are the steps to take:

1. Analyze the work to be done
2. Determine the elements of marketing needed
3. Design individual positions
4. Document the proposed structure
5. Communicate and implement the structure

As in so many human activities in the business arena, there are several options in organizing to accomplish a task. In this chapter, we offer two such tools. The first is to analyze the task to be undertaken. The second is to design a structure to accomplish the task.

The Work to Be Done

Suppose we are to determine a forecast of future work requirements. This involves examining current work and anticipating future requirements as dictated by projected change. We must also inventory current work and forecast which activities are to be continued and which new ones are to be added.

Here are some considerations that contribute to the analysis:

- Instances where work will be purchased from outside sources
- Work-process flow charts to clarify requirements and relationships
- Determining work to be done centrally and work to be dispersed to other sites or plants
- Projects of magnitude, such as new product lines, market development programs, or building new distribution channels
- The span of the marketing manager's job as to those functions that report in
- An inventory of demanding or complex decisions, to determine responsibility/authority positioning
- Unusual technical, promotional, and educational activities required

Criteria for Work Analysis

Here are some critical questions that can facilitate work analysis:

- Is all essential marketing work included?
- Is all of the work essential?
- Is all of the work really marketing work?
- Are the positions included adequate to match up with the needs of the other functions in the business?
- Can we provide needed services in a timely fashion?
- Have we covered all the product lines, market segments, distribution channels, and plant and site locations?

Establishing the Structural Form

The variations and combinations available to create a structure for marketing are almost infinite. We can narrow the choices by suggesting five types of organizational structure suitable for selection or refinements.

The Key Elements of Structure

- Product lines, salable services, and brands offered
- Markets or market segments to be served
- Sales and service channels
- Marketing functions, including work to be shared with other units or purchased externally
- Area and geographical considerations

Also to be considered are the distinctions of different types of businesses, such as service enterprises, distribution-centered companies, and franchises.

We must search for balance among the elements. In some cases, attention needs to be on the marketing functions, in others on product lines, markets served, or distribution channels.

We propose seeing structure from the point of view of the marketing manager as having a dual focus on objectives and strategies and on the work inventory to be accomplished.

Criteria for Evaluating Structures

1. Does the structure meet customer-convenience and other marketplace requirements?
   Test: Will it provide for customer service, market coverage, and distribution suitability as well as provide competitive advantage?
2. Will the structure achieve the objectives and strategies of the marketing operation?
   Test: Is it forward-looking? Can we define objectives and strategies for each component?
3. Is there a place for each component in the work inventory?
   Test: Are all marketing functions assigned? Are all product lines, markets, and distribution channels employed?

4. Is the structure compatible with the style of the company?

   Test: Will it enhance the working climate in terms of employee morale, motivation, and performance?

5. Will it provide proper emphasis and balance?

   Test: Are planning and day-to-day operating needs given essential emphasis? Are short- and long-range considerations in balance? Are all marketing functions covered equitably? Are profit and growth goals in balance?

6. Does the structure meet relationship requirements?

   Test: Can decision authorities be clearly defined? Will the integration of effort and teamwork be facilitated between marketing and other functions?

7. Are supervision and control requirements met?

   Test: Are the purpose and scope of each component manageable? Can the manager cope with the number and variety of reporting positions?

8. Is the human component properly considered?

   Test: Can the structure be staffed? Does it permit performance evaluation? Does it facilitate training and development?

9. Are the various systems built into the structure so they operate in an integrated manner?

   Test: Is there provision for product teams where appropriate? Will sales, advertising, and other promotional activities integrate effectively?

10. Is the overall structure simple, clear to all, and unified?

Part Three

Orienting Strategic Planning to the Marketplace

10

Strategic Planning From a Marketing Point of View

We need to ask a series of questions about an organization to determine the basis and the direction of the strategic planning process.

1. Does the business focus inwardly or outwardly? Inward is on technologies, production facilities, and financial resources. Outward is on the marketplace and competition.

2. Is the company present-oriented or future-oriented? Present-oriented focuses on the solution of existing problems, present market share, and near-term financial return. Day-to-day operational expediency governs. Future-oriented focuses on identifying and creating opportunities at longer range.

3. Are distinct business and market segments defined for planning purposes? Or is the business as a whole the essential planning view?

Marketing's Role in Planning

The answers to the questions above indicate the extent and depth of marketing's role and involvement in the strategic plan-

ning process. The degree to which the company focuses outwardly on the marketplace, demand, and customers' needs
and wants is directly connected to the desire for a marketing
point of view.

The marketing organization has a three-point role in planning:

1. To provide market-focused contributions and guidance
2. To develop marketing plans for implementation of the
   overall business plan
3. Integrating marketing plans with the efforts of other
   business functions

Every business entity plans in some form. Included here
are the inspiration-of-the-moment approach, the shoot-from-
the-hip type, and so on, right up to the highly systematized,
operations-research methods that explore all possible options.
There are at least four important options in the strategic planning process:

1. *Informal vs. formal planning.* Both processes are useful in
any business, but the extent to which each is to be emphasized
is a critical decision. Informal planning is by far the more common. It is expedient and seldom systematic. To a large extent,
it is reactive to short-range customer and competitor happenings in the marketplace. It is often not written and thereby carries that shortcoming. By contrast, formal planning has specific
procedures, clearly defined assignments, and schedules. Formal planning is by definition committed to the production of
written plans.

2. *Functional vs. business-entity planning.* Functional planning represents a plan stemming from each of the functions of
the business, that is, engineering, production, design, marketing, management information systems, and so on. It assumes
a separate planning activity by each. This approach carries the
drawback of needing extensive communication and integration
among planners and plans. Business-entity planning represents the whole business outlook and focuses on both the individual businesses or market segments of the company and

their markets. For planning purposes, all of the functions contribute to this integrated view. A by-product of this is an emphasis on teamwork with common written plans.

3. *Operational vs. strategic planning.* Operational planning focuses on continuation or expansion of present activities, either formally or informally. It tends to be short-range and expedient, with an emphasis on tactical moves and current profit. Strategic planning focuses on business opportunities, the future, and change. It considers alternative business and marketing objectives. It seeks a balance between profit and growth. It is formal planning and results in a written plan.

4. *Right-to-left vs. left-to-right planning.* Right-to-left planning focuses on resources and works from them toward the marketplace. It establishes general objectives and anticipates the organization's fulfilling them without particular regard to the specific situation. Left-to-right planning focuses on the marketplace and works backward toward the resources of the business. It starts with an estimate of the situation, considers market opportunities, calculates risk/reward relationships, and forecasts the probability of success. It provides for deployment and modification of resources to accomplish the goals set forth.

As we develop it here, the approach to planning makes choices between each of these alternatives. It selects formal over informal, business-entity over functional, strategic over operational, and left-to-right over right-to-left planning. By virtue of these selections, we necessarily cast a vote for a systematic process and for written plans.

Planning Nomenclature

It seems advisable to offer a simple glossary of important terms and concepts that are part of the planning process.

Purpose. Why the enterprise was created, exists, and is continued

Policy. The internal principles and rules that govern the operation of the company

Planning.   The system to formulate objectives, strategies, and courses of action and to establish a basis for resource allocation

The plan.   The official document in which management records and communicates the output of the planning process for implementation by the organization

Objective.   What is to be accomplished; the end result sought (marketing objectives include expanding the market, increasing market share, and contributing to profitability)

Strategy.   How objectives are to be accomplished; the means selected for implementing objectives

Course of action.   A statement that combines an objective with the strategy to accomplish it; the communication of what is to be done and how it will be done

11

An Intelligence System

Much of the mystery and confusion that surrounds the term *marketing* stems from the lack of factual information produced to properly inform management. Management has a real handicap to competitive performance when marketplace data about opportunities and problems are inadequate.

Intelligence systems have been developed to fill these needs in an orderly and consistent manner. Intelligence information must be developed from events occurring in the marketplace. Because of their outward orientation, marketing people are eminently suited to direct and staff this important function.

Commercial Intelligence

An effective intelligence system gathers and processes information about:

Customers
Markets
Competition
Environment

All of this has a single direction and purpose: successful prediction, both short- and long-term. The fear of the unknown, the future, has haunted humankind from its beginnings. Gathering and processing intelligence information is designed to permit business to peer further into the future and prepare itself to cope with circumstances not yet known.

The Bloodbath in Market Research

Marketing researchers are still telling the tale of Pillsbury's cake mix. In the late 1950s, Pillsbury developed a recipe that required the consumer to add only milk to the mix. The product bombed. Researchers rounded up housewives, interviewed them, and concluded that by giving the housewives too little to do, the mix made them feel useless. Once the user could add an egg to the mix, sales took off.

Modern-day market researchers smile indulgently about such homely, outdated methods in a time when high-powered computers and complex surveys are the vogue.

However, research revenues have continued to decline annually in the last several years. Researchers fear a rise in skepticism about the growing complexity of their craft. Many top executives are bewildered by the technical nature of research methods and the proliferation of consumer surveys.

Even more troubling are questions about the industry's track record. Many marketers say that, despite all of the advances, researchers often do an inadequate job of identifying their client's customers.

Several trends have coalesced to undermine the reputation of research. The validity of surveys is being jeopardized by the growing refusal of Americans to participate. The effect is to skew results by leaving out a sizable chunk of the market.

More sophisticated research methods have had their share of problems as well. Since the early 1980s, researchers have been making more and more recommendations for new products based on the results of surveys and computer-generated scenarios for different marketing strategies. The trouble is, these scenarios don't always take all of the crucial factors into account.

We all know of successful companies that seem suddenly to take a downturn in their market position, or that bank too long on past successes. "If it ain't broke, don't fix it," so commonly heard, presumes something that is likely not so. It presumes that the future will be as the past has been.

The fact that it "ain't broke" today says nothing about tomorrow and its needs and circumstances.

Humankind has been very thorough in its documentation of its past, its history. Another simplistic presumption is that history repeats itself. History may repeat itself if all else remains constant. But we see very few situations in modern business life in which we could fairly say that there are many constants.

So intelligence gathering and processing is vital in preparing management for the future actions and adjustments it will be taking.

Intelligence focuses on:

Customers
Markets
Competition
Environment

What follows is an elaboration on the subcategories of these basic areas.

1. Customers' opinions and attitudes
   • Company policies
   • Products
   • Sales service
   • Availability and delivery
   • Service and warranties
   • Pricing
   • Promotion and merchandising
   • Credit and collection
2. Markets
   • Size
   • Location
   • Composition
   • Geography
   • Demography
   • Distribution

3. Competition
   - Policies
   - Products
   - Pricing
   - Market strategies
   - Sales and distribution
   - Promotion and merchandising
   - Service
4. Environment
   - Economic conditions
   - Social conditions
   - Political conditions
   - Technological change

Information Sources

In the selection of sources, there is tremendous variance from industry to industry. Distinctions between product lines and service offerings preclude listing sources here. Suffice it to say that focusing on the kinds of information needed will ultimately determine the sources to be cultivated in the gathering process.

Constant and consistent monitoring procedures are the issue. The first step is to designate responsible individuals to focus on particular segments. Next, we establish a system for forwarding information collected by these individuals, along with the criteria for formatting this information. Then, we create a medium for processing and circulating information to those in need of it.

Let us keep in mind that information is not intelligence. Missing is evaluation of the significance of the data, judging the necessary timing, and measuring the effect of any change on the several functions within the company. Remember our earlier point: The purpose of all of this complex activity is forecasting and predicting the future. Above all, we must remember the "ripple effect," when change is made in one policy or function in a complex organization. There are few isolates in modern business. Interrelationship is the watchword.

The last step in converting data into intelligence is to communicate it. Of concern here are both the message and the medium for delivering it. We all know that there are myriad ways we can deliver any one message. The balance sheet and graphic media are but two of many choices for communicating. In this case, we allow the message to determine the medium. Clarity, simplicity, impact, speed, and accuracy of the processing procedures are our guides.

Communicating Intelligence

Selectivity is an important concept in communicating data and intelligence to the company. We must exercise selectivity as to:

- Who gets the information?
- What form should it take?
- Why do they need to know it?
- How are they expected to use it?

The ultimate value of intelligence is twofold: in the lead time it affords the company for strategic planning, and in the reaction time advantages it brings. Care must also be taken to protect this information from leaks and misuses. Disseminating information on a need-to-know basis helps provide security.

Feedback

A system should be established to create a flow of feedback evaluation from the recipients of the information to the providers of it. This assures that what is transmitted (as well as how it is transmitted) continues to be what the users need and want.

As in any human affairs, projects begin to take on a life of their own. Files and procedures have been known to continue far beyond their useful life because there was no feedback system provided to constantly monitor, refine, and adapt the intelligence to the company's needs. Here are a few guidelines for an intelligence system:

1. Make sure it provides for day-to-day operational requirements, as well as for planning purposes.
2. Tap significant sources regularly and use secondary sources and special studies as needed. Don't allow the source bank to become stale and repetitive.
3. Keep the system totally legal and ethical in its methods and sources.
4. Keep the system as simple as possible. The desire to elaborate is another human attribute that we should avoid.
5. Remember that intelligence is the raw material of planning and decision making; it must be made available in usable form as quickly as is feasible.

Intelligence on Competitors

Some guidelines on studying competitors are also useful. Proper subjects for monitoring include:

- Production—current output, capacity, and facilities
- Inventories—finished, in process, and in distribution
- Costs—production, distribution, and service
- Profits—current, past, and trends
- Organization—present, structural, and staffing changes
- Products—current designs, modifications, new introductions, competitive ratings
- Customer relations—consumer reports, opinion surveys
- Finance—resources, borrowings, liquidity
- Growth—internal generation, acquisition, divestiture

Again, we accentuate that only legal and ethical sources should be tapped. There is plenty of information available from trade sources, common customer bases, distributors, and the trade press, all of whom can be identified and cultivated. Any other methods fall under the heading of espionage, a very serious charge which has extralegal implications.

Examples of Intelligence Work

Utilizing an opinion survey, a business equipment manufacturer was able to determine that in a large segment of the potential customer base the initial impetus for buying new equipment was not from management, middle management, or the purchasing department. Rather, it was machine operators who critiqued the equipment presently available and specified the alterations needed. These machine operators at the bottom of the normal influence chain were, in fact, the prime movers and ultimate decision makers on these major purchases.

A manufacturer of computer equipment tipped its hand on some design specs when an R&D person, presenting a paper at a technical meeting, inadvertently disclosed the direction to be taken with a proposed new line.

Through intelligence gathering, a manufacturer of refrigerators intending to enter the French market uncovered the fact that most wine bottles used in that country were of greater height than expected. The appliance maker was able not only to design shelf height to accommodate this but was able to turn it into a product feature in the promotion.

Marketing Research Among the CEOs

When given the statement "More often than not, the information produced by focus-group research is as accurate and useful as the results of survey research at less than half the cost," CEOs proved to be amazingly misinformed about focus groups.

In fact, 38 percent didn't know whether the statement was true or false. Of the CEOs polled, 36.3 percent felt it was probably true, 13.4 percent thought it was probably false, and 4.9 percent said it was definitely true. Only 5.3 percent answered that it was definitely false—which it is.

Only 4.1 percent knew it was true that: "Generally speaking, a firm should not allocate a high share of its research budget to focus interviews."

Focus-group research has value from the perspective of

giving insight into the language that consumers use, but it has no value when it comes to helping companies make multimillion-dollar decisions.

No one has any idea how representative a focus group may be. After all, many researchers today conduct focus groups [only] among people who have time to participate. We have said, half seriously, most focus groups are made up of semicomatose people with time on their hands who are roaming through shopping malls searching for some excitement. . . . These are not representative samples.[1]

[1]Kevin J. Clancy and Robert S. Shulman, *The Marketing Revolution: A Radical Manifesto for Dominating the Marketplace* (New York: HarperCollins, 1992).

12

Market Segments

We need to define the term *market segments* in order to provide a sound and consistent basis for strategic planning for the company. Few businesses are homogeneous in the areas of customers, products and services, sales and distribution, and competition. Most large enterprises are quite diverse in these regards. This diversity requires us to be able to differentiate among the objectives and strategies appropriate for different parts of the enterprise.

In the planning process, companies select from among the following factors for their planning process:

Units of organization
Accounting classifications
Organizational function
Product lines

We suggest the use of the term *business arena*. This is any market in which a business participates that has a set of customers with common requirements and a set of known competitors. When we understand each arena, we can define the market segments that focus our strategic and marketing planning.

Key Arena Factors

First we identify those factors that shape the market. The following are key questions to ask:

- Who are our present and potential customers?
  - What are the needs and wants of these groups?
  - What are the consumers' lifestyles, attitudes, and opinions?
  - What are their purchasing policies and influences?
  - How do they view us?
  - How are they changing?
- Present and potential markets
  - Are the markets clearly classified?
  - Are the persuasive approaches for each clearly classified?
  - Are our intelligence system and market research providing the facts and insights we need?
  - Are our industry and sales forecasts adequate for planning purposes?
  - Have we used test marketing effectively?
- Current and future products and services
  - Where do we stand in product leadership?
  - What are the trends?
  - How do we rate in product acceptance, preference, and demand?
  - Is our product and service planning meeting the needs of changing markets?
- Present and anticipated competition
  - Do we know the strengths and weaknesses of those with similar products and services?
  - Are we aware of who else is serving the same end users with different means and products and services?
  - Are we aware of those entering from different industries?
  - Are we up-to-date on the effect of competitive activities in the marketplace, including new offerings, pricing, promotion, and other strategies?
- Strategic emphasis
  - Do we have a clear, unambiguous sense of our strategic history, knowing what has worked well and why?
  - Have we fit the proposed strategies to specific market segments?

- —Are our present moves and countermoves appropriate to changing market conditions?
- —Are we successful in anticipating and countering the strategic actions of our principal competitors?
- Sales and distribution channels
  - —Are our product and market assignments clearly designated and appropriate to each channel?
  - —Are these assignments suited to changing market conditions?
  - —Does our distribution system reach far enough into the marketplace to exploit all opportunity profitably?
  - —Are we initiating distribution innovations and trends, or following them?
  - —Is our performance in each channel what it should be? Are we optimizing our penetration?
- Persuasion tools and methods
  - —Do we have the right mix of sales, advertising, promotion, and merchandising tools to suit each market?
  - —Are our persuasive tools seen to be effective by customers? Are they used effectively by our sales and distribution personnel and by those in a position to recommend our products or services to users?
- Ability to serve
  - —Do we have the capability to serve our customers' needs and wants?
  - —Are our customer services adequate? Are our customers willing to pay for them?
  - —Are our R&D manufacturing/production facilities capable of serving our customers' product and service demands?
- Environmental forces
  - —Are we aware of changes, current or impending, in the business climate with respect to economic conditions, social trends, and political and governmental influences?
- Company vision and image
  - —Are our policies and practices appropriate to present market conditions? Are we communicating the company personality and character effectively?

—Are we gaining or losing in public acceptance?
—Do we know the impact of public attitudes and opinions on sales of our products?

These questions should be answered by an intelligence system that is being effectively operated. If this is not so, then it is a clear signal of the need to modify and expand the intelligence gathering system to the point that it can contribute answers to these questions.

Evaluating Significant Arena Factors

Effective evaluation of each significant arena factor requires examination from several perspectives. Experience provides at least a dozen methods for simplifying and facilitating the work.

1. *Employ a triple time focus.* Look back to identify factors that have had a major influence in the past. Look around you to select the present factors that determine the market struc-

---

The Wall Street Journal reports that some very successful companies in the catalog business are encountering difficulty as they try to expand beyond catalog sales into retail outlets.

Royal Silk, a very successful mail-order supplier of silk blouses and dresses, has filed for bankruptcy, saying its entry into retail stores has been disastrous.

Several other mail-order companies are having trouble becoming storefront successes. Sharper Image Corp., originally a catalog retailer selling an eclectic array of upscale merchandise to the affluent, blamed rapid expansion and greater-than-expected declines in its catalog as two factors contributing to declining revenues.

Sharper Image, Williams-Sonoma Inc., Shopsmith Inc., and Brookstone Co. are finding that expansion into retail stores brings a series of unexpected problems.

"Catalog companies get into trouble running retail stores because they don't recognize the two businesses are distinctly different," says Maxwell Sroge, an industry consultant.

Source: Reprinted from *The Wall Street Journal,* © Dow Jones & Company, Inc., 1989. All rights reserved.

ture. Look ahead to anticipate factors that will shape the situation to be faced.

2. *Select appropriate time spans.* There is a temptation to select a single time span for everything. This is because symmetry seems to offer some advantage. The time span selected is commonly five to ten years, as much planning literature suggests. We disagree strongly. We stand for selecting a time span that meets the reality of a particular business and its elements. For example, facility commitments in heavy industry manufacturing must embrace a twenty- or twenty-five-year period. Technical development or sales-force requirements may need only consider a five- to ten-year period. By contrast, a housewares business may require looking ahead only one to three years.

3. *Differentiate stable from dynamic elements.* In every arena there are relatively stable factors, changing slowly if at all. There are others that by nature shift rapidly with changes in economic and environmental conditions. Sorting these out permits emphasis on the predominant dynamic elements. We still need frequent appraisal of factors classified as stable, to continue to make sure that deviations are not occurring.

4. *Recognize dominant factors.* We must isolate dominant factors that are the primary determinants of success or failure. For example, in introducing new technical products or features, top market position may be gained by getting the jump on competitors. So in this example speed of innovation has great leverage and impact. Or in introducing a new packaged grocery product, the impact of heavy brand promotion may be the determinant.

5. *Employ several points of view.* Additional perspectives and new insights may be provided by considering each factor from various points of view. For example, market trends, product acceptability, and price-change reactions should usually be examined from customer, sales force, distributor, and marketplace competitor positions to minimize any biases and assure objectivity.

6. *Identify relationships and patterns among the factors.* Many arena factors are so interrelated that changes in magnitude or

direction in one have an important bearing on others. Identification of these relationships will help to determine intelligence requirements. For example, consumer movements in certain markets may determine whether to introduce new environmental controls, or whether to use a given type of distribution.

7. *Examine combinations of factors.* When viewed separately, a single change in market conditions or a minor shift in the business environment may seem to be innocuous. However, changes in several minor factors of small significance may combine to have a major impact in the marketplace. For example, taken separately, recent changes in attitudes and lifestyles of young people appear to have little market significance. Yet, when viewed in the light of a combination of social, economic, and political considerations, they have had great impact and relevance for many businesses.

8. *Separate facts from opinions.* Both facts and opinions are essential for perceptive analysis. But when the two are mixed indiscriminately even the experienced analyst may get confused. Where possible, use a simple code to differentiate the degree of precision existing in estimates and forecasts. This is a convenient way to differentiate facts from opinions.

9. *Separate adjustable factors from fixed.* Some factors in the marketplace are immutable aspects of the business and not likely to change. Others are subject to influence by shifts in policy, strategy, or other factors. Planning and decision making are facilitated when these two situations are clearly differentiated. For example, in a given market, one form of distribution may be so firmly established that no single competitor can depart effectively from that approach. On the other hand, a new distribution approach may be well received where no single, fixed pattern exists. Recognition of these situations is mandatory in the planning process.

10. *Get to the heart of the problems.* In analyzing market situations, symptoms are often confused with problems. To distinguish them clearly requires asking the right questions, conducting pointed inquiries in the field, analyzing all available intelligence, and above all, identifying the key roadblocks to solutions. For example, a tough competitive situation may ap-

pear to be caused by price cutting, while closer examination reveals that shortcomings in the product, poor service, or a weak selling program is the main failure.

11. *Question all assumptions.* Strategic planning rests heavily on assumptions. Often facts are in short supply when objectives and strategies are formulated. While some assumptions are grounded on verifiable observations, others are necessarily speculative and tentative. It is particularly important to reevaluate those assumptions that can be seen to be resting on shaky ground.

12. *Beware of impending-disaster factors.* Thorough analysis in the arena includes a constant search for major changes in market conditions, shifts in competition from unrecognized quarters, unpredictable technological changes, and other unexpected and "impossible" happenings. If such happenings *do* occur, they might be disastrous. Such events, recorded throughout business history, have destroyed major concerns or entire industries. While business planning cannot be omniscient, one of its essential duties is contingency planning, especially where the risks are great.

Selecting and evaluating key factors in the business arena provides the understanding essential for classifying and appraising the approaches we are presently using in persuasive activities and modifying them to suit changed requirements. Of course, this process may call for developing new approaches. This kind of analysis also generates information and insights for other steps in strategic planning.

Determining Suitable Persuasion Approaches

Most businesses have many options in deciding what markets they serve, what products and services they offer, and how they take these offerings to market. Great attention is given to rational selection of markets through market analysis, and to rational selection of offerings through product planning. Too often, though, the determination of how the offering will be taken to market is not given similar systematic attention.

All too often, past company practices, established industry practices, and even the whims of management prevail in establishing persuasion approaches.

This lack of concentrated attention to persuasion alternatives leads to the use of generalized approaches that may be suitable for only one aspect of a business.

A persuasion approach is defined as the basic method employed to reach customers having common requirements in a selected business arena.

This approach is determined by:

- The nature of the product or service
- The customer classification
- The type of purchase being made
- The sales and distribution channels used

These characteristics may vary greatly with a single product line being promoted in different market segments. For example, a line of industrial hardware may be offered to customers in a wide spectrum of industries. The purchasing points and customs may vary greatly. The channels may be direct, or indirect through jobbers, agents, distributors, and dealers. We will treat this in greater depth in Chapter 18, "Managing the Persuasion System."

Business Segmentation

There are many ways of dividing a business enterprise for the process of organizing, planning, accounting, or other operations. Among the most common are decentralization into:

- Product or profit centers
- Market or channel components
- Geographical regions or facilities

These distinctions influence the framework for planning. Our concern, however, is to identify and define business segments for strategic planning. Although there are advantages to having planning segments coincide with organization components, this should not be an overriding factor.

Planners can use product lines as segments when there are discrete markets, sales channels, and no complicating regional or facilities considerations. Planners must be careful to accommodate changes as they occur.

Where the business situation is more complex, a more sophisticated process of defining segments is essential for effective strategic planning. We recommend the following approach.

The Business-Segmentation Process

This is a three-dimensional approach that provides a basic framework for defining and describing business segments. The three elements are:

1. Activities—covering the range of work to be undertaken for the business segment
2. Products—covering the range of products and services to be offered to the markets in the business segment
3. Markets—relating to the range of customer classes to be served by the business segment

These three statements of scope provide a precise definition of the business segment. The equation of a business segment says:

scope of the activities + products for sale = markets

Table 1 considers a hardware business offering a wide range of products and related services to consumer, commercial, and industrial markets. It employs a variety of distribution channels and faces several major competitors.

Note that clearly in the several segments shown business and marketing objectives and their accompanying strategies vary substantially for each segment.

Segment 1. The primary objective for this basic consumer business may be to increase market share through a predomi-

Table 1.   Defining business segments for a hardware manufacturer.

Activities	Products	Markets
1. Developing, producing, and marketing	Standard bolts, nuts, screws	Consumers, through two-step distribution: jobbers and dealers
2. Procuring and marketing	Standard washers	Consumers, through two-step distribution: jobbers and dealers
3. Producing and marketing	Specialty bolts designed for customers	Automotive-parts distributors
4. Developing, producing, and marketing	Standard nuts and bolts	Original-equipment manufacturers
5. Producing and marketing	Specialty bolts designed for customers	Original-equipment manufacturers
6. Special technical services	Bolts designed for unique applications	Defense-system manufacturers

nant push-through strategy to gain maximum jobber and dealer representation.

Segment 2. The objective here is to round out the hardware line by adding washers produced by other manufacturers because dealers or jobbers demand complete line service. This is done for either of two reasons: first, because that is essential to the push-through strategy, and second, because there is simply an opportunity for additional profit through an established market.

Segment 3. In contrast, this specialized business emphasizes a direct profitability objective because of its outstanding production capability and efficiency.

Segment 4. The objective is to increase market share

through a strategy of pricing based on cost and an emphasis on quality control, cost reduction, and on-time delivery.

Segment 5. The predominant objective is to strengthen relationships with existing customers to get more of the standard-line business. Pricing based on cost and a customer-service strategy would work here.

Segment 6. This is included to show salable services treated as a product for a separate business segment. The objective here is market expansion, to build a new, highly technical hardware business. Technical customer service is the predominant strategy.

We intend this analysis to demonstrate that both business and market planning must be done for each business segment, as well as for the enterprise as a whole. Unless the activity, product, and market dimensions are clearly defined in their relationships to one another by breaking things down into distinct business segments, planning ends up dealing with conglomerate situations. In that case, objectives and strategies are so generalized that they become statements of philosophy. They also may be appropriate for only a portion of the business.

Market Segmentation

The practice of dealing with business segments provides an essential stage of refinement for planning.

However, in most businesses there is a need for an even sharper focus. This is provided by clear and perceptive market segmentation. This process of defining market segments contributes to effective classification of business segments as well. Accordingly, it is useful to view these two processes as interdependent steps in the work of strategic planning.

Definition

A market segment is defined as a group of customers with similar or related characteristics who have common needs and wants and who respond to the same motivation.

There is nothing static about this process. Markets are constantly segmenting and resegmenting themselves. With growth in size and complexity, markets change as customer and competitive forces alter their composition. Thus, it is necessary to redefine market segments regularly to be sure that the assumptions on which planning is based continue to square with reality in a changing arena.

Much of the continuing mystique surrounding marketing stems from failure to recognize and deal precisely with specific market segments.

No business can be all things to all customers. Even department stores and supermarkets must choose which customers they serve, what products they offer, and what services they provide. Similarly, the largest of automobile manufacturers must still break down the total car market into manageable segments and decide how to approach each one.

A nominally full-line electrical manufacturer offers only selected products and serves limited markets with many of them. Decisions must be made about what to include and what to omit. To put it another way: "How shall we segment the market?"

These decisions about which markets to serve and which to emphasize demand systematic identification procedures, evaluation of alternatives, and clear classification of market segments.

Ways to Segment a Market

Consumer markets may be segmented by:

- Geographic areas or neighborhoods
- Age groups
- Education
- Income levels
- Family size
- Lifestyles
- Product prices

Industrial markets segment by:

- Industries served
- Geographical considerations
- Technologies
- Distribution channels

Customer needs and wants are the primary considerations in any approach to market segmentation. Customers do not all want the same things from a product. Commercial and industrial customers seek products to suit the economic, technical, and other requirements of their enterprises. Different customer groups demand differing levels of service as well.

To define the market segments for the business, the strategic planner must discover these patterns and distinctions. The goal is to know in advance which group of customers responds to a given product or service and how many customers there are in each group.

A related task is to identify and analyze competitors' market segments. As a planner, you must gather information about their views of markets to gain a fuller understanding of your competitive arena, to comprehend their objectives, to anticipate their strategic moves. Market segmentation permits you to define your competition more clearly.

Market segmentation means discovering the parts of a market that have exploitable differences in their requirements, selecting those parts in which to excel and designing products and services to gain competitive advantage in the segments selected. Unless you do such segmentation, you leave effective product and service differentiation to chance.

This differentiation is accomplished by developing salable and promotable differences between your offerings and those of your competitors in a given market segment. Advantages may be in:

- Features
- Performance
- Quality
- Value

Similarly, service differentiation might be in:

- Availability
- Delivery
- Installation
- Warranties
- Training

One of the real challenges to the planner is to determine how many customers will buy an anticipated offering. Will there be enough to justify the expense of development and production? The accuracy of these forecasts directly relates to management's ability to predict failure or success.

Can older products be modernized or otherwise renewed? Can they be changed to fit into evolving or new market segments? What new products or services should be created to fit market segments? Which products or services should be eliminated because they no longer fit customer requirements or cannot stand up to competitive pressures?

Technical Innovation

With the increasing cost of research and development activities and the widening spectrum of technical possibilities, such efforts must be directed selectively to market segments where the potential for payoff is high. The critical decision of where, when, and how to innovate screams out for market-based direction. Astute selection of market segments is the key to sound decisions.

The Market-Segmentation Process

While there are variations in the nature and character of each market, these generalized steps hold up well as a process for analyzing each business segment:

1. Classify customers by basic needs and wants, utilizing product, price, and value factors in your business.

2. For each class of customers in step 1, identify the advantages and benefits sought.
3. Select the characteristics of each market served. For consumer markets, these may be age groups, income levels, family size, lifestyles and demographic considerations. For industrial markets they include size, location, competition, and distribution channels.
4. Denote environmental influences for each market, including economic, social, political, and physical factors.

An Example of Market Segmentation

This example is taken from the electrical housewares manufacturing business that produces three types of products: food preparation, personal care, and home comfort.

Step 1. Customer needs and wants. Customers need products for food preparation: toasters, coffee makers, food processors, juicers, can openers, beaters. Customers need products for personal care: hair dryers, shavers, hair curlers. Customers need products for home comfort: air conditioners, fans, heaters, dehumidifiers. Note that the differing needs and wants in each category affect the definition of a market segment.

Step 2. Advantages and benefits. Food-preparation products emphasize convenience, economy, and improved meals. Personal-care products emphasize improved personal appearance. Home-comfort products emphasize comfort and health.

Step 3. Significant market characteristics. Food preparation considers family size and lifestyle. Personal care considers such characteristics as age groups and income levels. Home care products are affected by geographical areas and other physical factors.

Step 4. Environmental influences. In the food-preparation products market, economic considerations weigh heavily. For personal-care products, social conformity and competition are important. For home-comfort products, physical factors such as weather and pollution are critical determinants.

If we were to approach planning for the housewares business as a whole instead of through segments, we would lack precision about customer needs, benefits sought, significant market characteristics, and other considerations in each of the three parts of the business.

While planning must ultimately be done for the whole business and for each product line, an approach like the one used here that focuses on such carefully selected market segments will yield more-precise information.

13

Formulating Objectives and Strategies

If we had to express the objectives of a business in one word, we would choose *more*. The pressure on all of our business organizations is for more volume, more profit, more growth, more cost reduction, more turns of inventory, and on and on. The problem comes when this pressure is for *all* of these—and all at the same time.

The Need for Selectivity

This all-at-once approach ignores the need for selectivity and discrimination. It fails to provide plausible courses of action that are practical, rational, and above all, achievable.

Probably the most critical decision is choosing between current profit and the reinvestment of earnings to achieve future growth and, eventually, longer-range profit. Another choice to be made is in seeking to expand the market for your product or service or moving to increase market share. In decisions between current profit and growth, the objectives and strategies must be made clear to all concerned lest there be confusion and people or functions working at cross purposes.

Let's look at a food manufacturer, for example. With one of its divisions, the cracker group, the choice might be made to keep its well-established brands yielding an excellent profit from a favorable price level and good turnover of inventory.

At the same time, the cookie group may lack adequate volume for optimal operation. Here they may choose to build volume through a program of promotions, couponing, price inducements, special features, and/or all of the above. One would be choosing to expand market share to achieve volume, but thereby sacrificing short-term profit for growth.

The point here is that these decisions should be made on a product-group basis. Most importantly, everyone involved in product development, marketing, support activities, sales, finance, and other functions must clearly understand the direction the group is to take.

This fundamental approach is also applicable to a retail chain. The management of the organization recognizes that objectives and strategies must fit the conditions found in each market in which the chain operates. Management at the regional and store levels develops objectives and strategies attuned to market conditions. These obviously vary from region to region and store to store. The key here is that market conditions are made an important basis of planning for the entire chain. This is also an excellent example of bottom-up planning and forecasting.

Broad areas of concern to top management that require constant vigilance and making choices are:

- Scope of the business—which segments of our business should we continue, drop, or enter?
  Choice of strategies:
  —Expand present business segments
  —Develop new segments
  —Eliminate segments no longer viable
  —Negotiate mergers, acquisitions, or joint ventures
- Business organization—is our management style, structure, and staffing appropriate? Is the choice between centralized and decentralized clear as it relates to each segment of the business?
  Choice of strategies:
  —Centralize or decentralize
  —Focus on products, markets, technologies, production, or geographic regions

- Performance evaluation—is our appraisal system attuned to our objectives and strategies and to any changes or adjustments that have been made? Have we provided for the distinctions between short- and long-range goals?
  Choice of strategies:
  —Short-term or long-term results
  —Current profit or future growth
  —Emphasis on economy or effectiveness

Concerns of marketers are understandably more focused on products and markets:

- Customer classes—where are our strengths and weaknesses? Are there changes or trends to monitor?
  Choice of strategies:
  —Focus broad or specialized classes of customers
  —Serve present customers or seek new ones
  —Serve many needs of a few customers or a few needs of many customers
- Competitors—are there vulnerabilities in their products, technologies, production, or distribution systems? Are there new people to watch?
  Choice of strategies:
  —Stress one's own strengths or competitors' weaknesses
  —Emphasize product, price, or customer service
  —Innovate or follow competitors in products or services
- Markets and distribution—in which lines should we seek increased share? Where to give it up or hold the line? Is our distribution system adequate for our plans for each line?
  Choice of strategies:
  —Market development in selected segments
  —Market-share growth in selected segments
  —Select distribution mode and channels
- Technology—are we adequately focused on new or modified products? Is redesign needed?
  Choice of strategies:
  —Stress high or low technology in products

      —Innovate or follow competitors
      —Emphasize product leadership in performance, features, and cost/price ratios
- Production capability—are we using outside sources and our own capabilities in proper balance? Are we at the right stage of automation?
Choice of strategies:
      —Emphasize cost or quality
      —Select inside or outside sources
      —Centralize production or decentralize it to market areas
- Finance—are we evaluating and adjusting our objectives for each segment as to return on investment, percentage of profit to sales, and cash-flow adequacy? Are changing conditions suggesting modifications?
Choice of strategies:
      —Report performance for individual segments or for the whole
      —Use a single performance standard for all segments or design a standard for each

Marketing Objectives and Strategies

Assuming that marketing in most organizations has at least three primary marketing objectives, we can examine courses of action for each.

    I. Enlarge the market
       A. By innovation or product development
          1. Improve existing products
          2. Develop new products
       B. By innovation or market development
          1. Develop present end-use markets
          2. Discover new end-use markets

Fortune magazine notes that marketers will have to learn some new rules. This has been brought about by the aging of the population, and by its changing ethnic composition.

As companies move away from strong dependence on a youth orientation, they have to create new approaches for older consumers.

The aging of the baby boomers and the growth of the senior population will leave fewer youngsters in its wake. Population growth in the United States has slowed to 0.9 percent a year, a trend that will continue throughout the 1990s.

Immigrants from Asia, Mexico, and Latin American countries will account for most of the growth because American women are bearing fewer children.

Led by the baby boomers—78 million strong, one-third of the population—U.S. consumers in the nineties will be older, richer, and harder for marketers to find. Consumer-goods companies will have to become more sensitive to distinctions of culture, and more dynamic in response to them.

Source: Christopher Knowlton, "Consumers: A Tougher Sell," *Fortune* (September 26, 1988), © 1988 Time Inc. All rights reserved.

II. Increase market share
    A. Emphasize product development or improvement
        1. Through product performance
        2. Through product quality
        3. Through product features
    B. Emphasize persuasion efforts
        1. Through sales and distribution
        2. Through advertising and promotion
    C. Emphasize customer service activities
        1. Through ready availability, order handling, and delivery
        2. Through credit and collection policies
        3. Through service after the sale

III. Improve profitability
    A. Emphasize sales volume
        1. Through sales and distribution effort
        2. Through advertising and promotion
        3. Through merchandising efforts

B. Emphasize elimination of unprofitable activities
   1. Prune product offerings and lines
   2. Prune sales coverage and distribution
   3. Prune customer services
C. Emphasize price improvement
   1. Initiate needed price increases
   2. Differentiate products and services from those of competitors
D. Emphasize cost reduction
   1. Improve marketing tools and methods in product planning, persuasive activities, and customer-service activities

As is often the case, the process of asking and answering these questions facilitates formulation of objectives and strategies. Having defined our market segments (Chapter 12), we can now concentrate on how to carry them out.

The four areas in which we determine our marketing emphasis are:

1. Product
2. Price
3. Persuasion
4. Customer service

These are our fundamental strategy alternatives. Each warrants separate attention as a basis for our decisions on marketing emphasis.

1. Product appeal
   • Offer a broad range of products, or offer a limited or selective range
   • Innovate with new products, or initiate changes in existing products, or follow competitors who lead in innovations
   • Introduce products with prompt profit payoff, or introduce products with greater long-term payoff

- Emphasize convenience, style, or appearance, or emphasize product functions and quality
- Stress product in the product/service package, or stress service
- Offer general-purpose products to suit a wide variety of uses, or offer specialized products for limited or special purpose

2. Price appeal
   - Take the lead in changing pricing policies, or follow competitors in making such changes
   - Price for immediate profit, or price for longer-range profit
   - Price for profit on the original sale, or price for profit on the follow-on sales
   - Choose high-risk–high-reward opportunities, or choose low-risk–low-reward opportunities
   - Price for direct sale, or price for lease, rental, or distributor sale

3. Persuasion effort
   - Use a direct-sales approach, or use agents, distributors, or dealers
   - Initiate changes in the persuasion approach, or follow changes initiated by competitors
   - Emphasize the sales effort, or emphasize the promotion effort
   - Employ a single unified approach for all sales channels, or employ diversified approaches for each sales channel
   - Establish a pull-through strategy to build customer acceptance and force distribution, or establish a push-through strategy to motivate distribution to carry the product and to move it

4. Customer service
   - Use a direct-to-customer service approach, or use an indirect approach via second parties
   - Initiate changes in customer-service approach, or follow changes in services initiated by competitors

- Provide widespread availability of your products, or provide limited availability through selective coverage
- Establish a liberal after-sale policy with generous warranties and returns of unsold goods, or establish a conservative after-sale policy to generate a profit on parts, replacement, and repairs
- Employ liberal credit, collection, billing, dating, and discounting policies, or employ a conservative policy

Marketing Expansion Through Product Development

Most managers think of direct sales or promotional activity when they seek to expand markets. It is easy to overlook another effective means for market expansion: the use of product innovation or development. This approach works for both existing and new product lines.

Existing Lines for Current Markets

First, consider an elastic market where use increases as cost of use decreases. (Price reduction also affects volume substantially.) Look for innovation opportunities to permit lower pricing by designing the product for lower costs of production, packaging, storage, transportation, or display.

For example, a manufacturer might standardize units for mass production. A container could be designed to serve as the package, display, and delivery unit. One might turn to miniaturization of components to reduce cost. The number of product units packaged for sale might be altered.

Similar opportunities may be found where the cost to the user is affected by factors beyond the price of the product. Use of the product may be expanded by reductions in related costs, such as reducing the costs of maintenance, service, installation, or display space. For example, designing elements of the product for easier and cheaper replacement improves product life and quality. Or consider encouraging present or new users to replace existing product because additional functions have been added.

New Product Lines for Unserved Markets

Look for occasions to innovate with your products to attract customers served by other industries. Here you could look for ways to exploit your special marketing and distribution capability. The focus could also be on innovation based on a new application of technology in which you are expert. A jet engine manufacturer might find applications in sewage treatment, or a chemical company might look to consumer detergents. An electronics manufacturer might look for opportunities to provide elements for the toy market.

The point to be appreciated is that marketing planners look at product development as well as market development for additional opportunity for their companies.

Formulating Objectives and Strategies

Certain principles and common procedures are available to assist in formulating objectives and strategies. Here is a list:

- Objectives are what is to be accomplished, the end result sought.
- Strategies are the "how" elements of planning, the means to the end.
- Courses of action are statements combining an objective with a strategy.
- Courses of action are needed for each business and market segment.
- Objectives and strategies need to be in harmony with each other.
- A predominant strategy should be selected for each business and market segment (see Table 2).
- Identify as many alternative strategies as possible for evaluation before final selection.

Table 2.   Contrasting strategy requirements.

Actions	Pull-through strategy	Push-through strategy
Objective	Seek competitive advantage through building brand acceptance and demand directly with the customer.	Seek competitive advantage by motivating distributors to carry and move your product.
Must do	Use media to promote image of brand. Maintain consistent program. Improve effectiveness of messages to customers. Price to cover services plus fair profit.	Provide incentives to stimulate volume selling. Strive for more and better outlets. Maintain standards of service consistent with company identity.
Might do	Force distribution through customer demand. Provide product availability so customer demand can be promptly satisfied. Use direct contact with distributors to assist sales.	Maintain superiority of selling assistance. Encourage commitment to your product and company objectives.
Don't do	Don't offer special prices to distributors continually as incentive to force inventory into distribution channels.	Don't price so distributor has too little profit. Don't overspend on advertising and promotion. Don't extend to distributors sales that stem from your direct-sales efforts.

- The guide for effective strategy selection is to make it practical, rational, and achievable.
- Three primary marketing objectives deserve constant attention: increasing market share, enlarging the market, and contributing to profitability.
- Objectives and strategies provide the basis for allocation of company resources.

14

The Strategic
Marketing Plan

There is hardly a business organization today that is not committed to the concept of strategic planning. It has become as much a part of the modern organization as the accounting function or the marketing function. Here we concentrate on that aspect of the overall strategic plan that is peculiarly and distinctively the responsibility of marketing.

While there is variation from company to company and industry to industry in the strategic planning process, most people agree that there are certain commonalities in the makeup of the business plan:

- The executive summary
- Analysis of the business arena
- Courses of action
- Sales budgets and resource allocation
- Performance evaluation

Since the marketing plan will grow out of the business plan, we follow this outline and use these categories as our main headings below.

Executive Summary

This part of the business plan is intended to provide to the general manager the substance of the proposed marketing plan. It emphasizes changes in the business arena observed by marketing and the principal courses of action recommended:

- Significant changes encountered in the business arena
- Principal courses of action
- Summary of sales budgets and marketing resource allocations
- Highlights of performance expectation and evaluation

Analysis of the Business Arena

This part reflects a thorough understanding and communication of the nature of the marketplace. Where there are changes in the definition of market segments, the reasons should be given here.

- Conditions, changes, and trends for each market segment and for the marketing operation as a whole
- The scope of markets, products and salable services, competition, strategic emphasis, sales and distribution channels, persuasion tools and methods, ability to serve, environment, and company vision and image
- Evaluation of the business arena for each market segment and for the marketing operation as a whole
- Economic, industry, and sales forecasts

Courses of Action

This is the heart of the plan, representing commitments by the marketing organization and guidance of the functions of the company in support of the marketing objectives. A calendar of major marketing programs should be included, showing targets, checkpoints, and the timing for each event.

- Marketing objectives and strategies for each market seg-

ment and the marketing operation as a whole, including time schedules and principal implementing assignments
- Market expansion plans, market share expectations, and relevant contribution to profitability
- The strategy for product appeal, price appeal, persuasion efforts, and customer service
- Specific courses of action for marketing to take in implementing overall business objectives and strategies
- Projects for exploration to identify and evaluate opportunities for innovation and development of new markets, products, and services

Sales Budgets and Allocations

The purpose here is to integrate budgets, expenses, and cost reductions into sales expectations, and to provide a foundation for performance evaluation.

- Highlight of sales budgets for each market segment and for the business as a whole: contingency alternatives and major project expectations
- Highlights of marketing expenses and capital budgets for each market segment and for the marketing operation as a whole
- Summary explanation for major changes in allocations compared with previous years
- Sales, marketing expense, and marketing capital budgets

Performance Evaluation

Here we are looking for harmonious, reinforcing qualitative and quantitative performance evaluations.

- Methods, standards, time periods, and other measures for evaluating market performance. Include product and market leadership, accuracy of the forecasting, expense controls, and cost reductions

Special care must be taken that one of the cardinal rules of management theory be applied in this planning stage as well: Authority and responsibility must be coterminous and coequal. As an example, marketing must not have profit responsibility if it does not have control of research and development and production.

We sometimes see blame placed on marketing for performance failures when the forecasts provided do not have sufficient accuracy. Some failures belong to production, as when product is not delivered on schedule. Troublesome pitfalls can sometimes be avoided by making assessments as projects progress.

Common Planning Pitfalls and Fallacies

The marketing manager needs to be alert to some common errors:

- Believing that planning eliminates risk
- Neglecting to modify the plan when conditions change
- Failing to provide contingency plans
- Not recognizing the strategic advantages of surprise in a competitive situation
- Not using strategic planning to provide equilibrium between opportunity and resources
- Failing to forfeit a losing battle soon enough
- Assuming that "crystal ball" forecasters have an adequate vision of the future
- Rejecting the reality that most sales forecasts are likely to prove wrong
- Forgetting that competitors who plan strategically are less vulnerable than those who do not

Communicating the Plan

Please remember that there is more to communication than distribution. Fancy binders containing elaborate plans are useless, of course, if they are lying on dusty shelves. A fine, thoughtful plan can be sabotaged if communication is inadequate. More people involved in this planning process usually means more people who will be receptive to and concerned about the plan.

Be certain that all those responsible for executing a portion of the plan receive at least that part of the plan, so that they know what is expected of them.

The marketing manager wants to be certain that those peers in other functions are aware of the portions of the marketing plan that affect their own function in some way.

Part Four

Operating a Dynamic Marketing System

15

Managing Change in Marketing

Why do some businesses fail while others survive and prosper? Analysis shows that the marketing-centered reasons are often inertia and worship of the status quo.

The expression we have heard before, "If it ain't broke, don't fix it," is sometimes the culprit. CEOs dealing with their marketers can be guilty of this kind of thinking. "This is what got us here" is not always a proper map for our route into the future.

Don't-rock-the-boat thinking does not deal with changes in the competitive arena, new competitors, or technological innovation. But these *are* factors that marketing must consider.

Managing change is a primary responsibility of marketing. A study of how organizations survive change demonstrates alertness to change, quick action, and astute innovation to take advantage of a changing scene.

To base decision making on tradition, habit, whim, default, or following competitors' leads is an open invitation to sluggish reaction to change. A dynamic marketing operation is one whose management looks to the future. Relentless attention is given to change in the marketplace, opportunities and necessities to innovate, and, above all, to the management of change.

It is essential to having an orderly approach to finding new product opportunities and new markets. In many industries, there is a steady flow of opportunities generated from within the business or from the outside.

Managing change is essentially dependent on the *processing* of opportunities rather than on simply having a dragnet out to find as many opportunities as possible. The task is to identify, evaluate, and select those few possibilities that have the best chance to pay off for your company.

The dynamic marketing organization takes the lead in selecting business opportunities. Here is a list of criteria for evaluating new products:

Market Opportunity

- How well does the product meet an identifiable customer need or want?
- What are the customer benefits and advantages of this proposed product?
- What is the anticipated customer acceptance?
- What is the nature, size, and anticipated growth rate of the market?
- What is the right timing for introduction of the product?
- What is the assessment of our ability to take on competition?
- What are the number and strength of competitors with similar products? With different products?

Ability to Serve

- Do we have the ability to develop an acceptable, competitive, salable product and innovate unique features?
- What are the barriers to entry, such as patents, licenses, and blocks to effective distribution?
- What are the resources requirements of capital, facilities, manpower, skills, sales and distribution, and services?
- Is our production capability adequate?

Anticipated Results

- What is expected profitability, cash flow, return on investment, and contribution to overhead?
- What is the volume of sales expected, and what impact will it have on other products and lines?

- What is the additional value of this new product as a lead to still others? Does it support existing product?
- What is the overall chance for success or failure?

It is well to remember that some observers estimate the failure rate of new products in the packaged consumer-goods business to be in excess of 95 percent. This speaks loudly to the need for more careful and thorough analysis and evaluation of new ventures. The cost of failure is financially and emotionally very high and thereby destructive. Much of this failure rate can and should be avoided.

Managing Change

Do you manage it, or are you swept along and managed by it? To paraphrase Alvin Toffler, change is a constant. Only the rate of change is not. It is, in fact, accelerating.

Customers are changing, markets are changing, products and services are changing, sales and service channels are changing, competition and the business environment are changing.

These conditions require the marketing function to get out in front of the organization and lead. There are several options to deal with change:

- Ignore it and chance death
- Study trends and adjust to them
- Anticipate events and move first
- Lead and make things happen

One approach to opening one's mind to the future is first to anticipate things that "cannot" happen to the company—and then think through what you would do if that came to be.

Think back relatively few years to those manufacturers and retailers who refused to acknowledge discount outlets as ever being part of the mainstream. Retailers did not react, and some manufacturers even refused to supply them. Such a sea change

One of the main reasons companies launch new market entries is to grow their revenues. Originally, most growth came from the growth of the product category. But today, instead of promoting real growth, new market entries appear to do little more than fractionate the market. Moreover, this fragmentation of the market has made many product categories susceptible to unwholesome price competition. By working harder than ever, the contemporary marketer often makes it impossible for many of them to succeed.

A few statistics suggest how dire this situation has become. An analysis of packaged-goods warehouse data indicates that of the tens of thousands of new product entries created in the preceding fifteen years, only 250, or substantially less than one percent, achieved wholesale sales volume of 15 million, which is the minimum most large manufacturers would regard as desirable to maintain an item in distribution and earn a worthwhile profit.

Astute new-product developers who simply said no to every idea, good or bad, would have a prodigious predictive record.

Certainly, new market entries are important to remain competitive, to defend against competitive attack, and to assure future growth—even if the odds of success are small. But considering the high failure rate, it is bizarre that so much time, money, and effort continue to be committed to the launch of new entries into the marketplace.

New products must be managed with a poker mentality, not a craps attitude. Craps is a game of pure chance; poker is a game of skill and tactics. New-product managers must fold their hand frequently—early in the game. Discipline is required until the right new market entry is at hand. To enhance the probability of winning, wait until the entry is truly superior to the products presently in the marketplace.

Source: Alvin Achenbaum, in *Marketing Review* (February 1993), American Marketing Association, New York Chapter.

could be on the horizon for your business. You must anticipate and therefore undertake contingency planning.

Forward-looking managers of change identify obstacles to change within their organization. The difficulty here is that these roadblocks are often emotional in nature. Listen to the voices of resistance to change:

"We've tried that before."
"We've never done that before."
"I know a company that tried that, and it failed."
"We've always done it this way."
"It's too radical."
"Why change? It's working okay."
"We've done okay with this."
"It's too much trouble."
"We're different than they are."
"We lack the authority to do this."
"Top management won't go for this."
"The troops won't buy it."
"The union will scream."
"Our customers won't like this."
"We don't have the time for this."
"We don't have enough help to do this."
"It costs too much."
"It will hurt the margins."
"It's not in the budget."
"We are not ready for this."
"Put it in writing, and we'll study it."
"We should test this first."
"Form a committee to study it."
"Let's think about it."
"Put it on the shelf for the time being."
"You're right, but . . ."
"Good idea, but it won't work."
"It can't be done."

Continuous Innovation

The marketing concept includes a dedication to continuous innovation in the business. Marketing is called upon to support, stimulate, encourage, and initiate innovation within the company. The challenge of innovation is to improve the link between the marketplace and the creative capabilities of the business. Marketing's involvement should assure that innovation fits the realities of customer acceptance, competitive considerations, and the profit and growth goals of the business. Opportunities for innovation include:

- New products and services
- Development and expansion of new markets
- New applications and uses
- Improved customer service
- New sales and service channels
- Pricing alternatives

Around the turn of the century, economists felt innovation was the root cause of economic growth and the entrepreneur was its primary agent. It is the marketing person who fulfills that role today.

The tools and methods of innovation are many. They range from serendipity—an aptitude for making fortunate discoveries—to modern computerized systems approaches. Heuristics, the study of methods of discovery and invention, has properly become a part of marketing development programs.

For most businesses, however, the most promising and rewarding approach to creative and systematic product planning is to have marketing lead the charge in tying innovative thinking and proposals to the marketplace.

The Systems Attitude and Approach

From its conception, the marketing concept suggested a more orderly and factual approach to serving customers. It has emphasized:

- Research into customers, markets, and distribution
- Forecasting of the economy, the industry, and sales
- Testing products and services before launch
- Analysis of sales, competition, and distribution performance

• Balancing customer needs with company considerations

Great progress has been made in using the tools of systems analysis and synthesis. These methods have resulted in broadening the term *market research* into *marketing research*, thus covering all aspects of the field. Such methods have provided an orderly approach for organization analysis and design. Principles have evolved for market-focused business information systems. They have facilitated an understanding of strategic planning, including the definition of market segments and targeted objectives. Also, a systematic process for appriasing marketing performance has stemmed from the use of these tools.

The marketing system can be examined in a number of ways. Traditionally, the focus was on product lines. Later, the emphasis shifted to markets and product-market classifications. Then there was a focus on functional analysis and functional organization. Following that was a concentration on market segments, including demography, environment, and lifestyles. From this evolution have come all of the essential ingredients for examination of the marketing process.

Our perspective sees the marketing process as three interrelated systems:

1. A product system
2. A persuasion system
3. A support system

Chapters 17 to 19 explore these subsystems and integrate them into the enlightened, always growing and changing marketing process.

16

Marketing for Service Industries

Marketing initially developed with the exchange of tangible products between customer and manufacturer as its primary goal. In the last thirty years or so, we have seen a major change in the nature of commercial output in the United States. Seventy percent of the gross national product now comes from the exchange of services, and this is forecast to continue to grow. Our economy has obviously experienced a radical change in the product-to-service ratio.[1]

Service: the Intangible Benefit

A *service* can be defined as any intangible benefit exchanged between two parties.

The term *services marketing* covers a very broad spectrum of organizations and businesses and the services they provide. Included here will be such nonprofit organizations as the U.S. Postal Service, educational institutions, care-givers, and charities, among many.

[1]See further three books on this subject: Karl Albrecht and Ron Zemke, *Service America* (Homewood, Ill.: Business One Irwin, 1985); Karl Albrecht, *At America's Service* (Homewood, Ill.: Business One Irwin, 1988); and Carole Congram and Margaret Friedman, *The AMA Handbook of Marketing for the Service Industries* (New York: AMACOM, 1991).

In the business sector, we have such services as transportation, the professions (law and medicine among others), automotive repair, health care, banking, and the hospitality industry, to mention only a few.

With many products there is, in fact, a mix of product and service that is obtained by the buyer. For example, the act of buying a product may also confer additional benefits of service: a guarantee, follow-up repair or adjustment, advice and support in the use of the product, or product-update information.

An Example of Intangible Benefit

While a book or other publication is seen at first as a product, its ultimate benefits are essentially intangible. The value derived from a book is in the form of information, education, entertainment, or some combination of them all. But this is an intangible benefit. Therefore, one can view a book as a service provided by the author and publisher to the buyer.

In some cases, the actual provider of the service confers the main benefit, as in the case of a noted surgeon or attorney. This is also true of performers in such areas as sports and entertainment.

Because many service firms are small, they tend not to use many marketing tools, contenting themselves with signage and

---

How is it that a start-up company like Dell Computer has been able to grow geometrically and at the expense of such icons of business as IBM and Digital Equipment? By putting the customer in the center of the company focus. By creating an atmosphere that says, "Your problem is our problem, your needs are our concern." And meaning it and living it every day.

This is most commonly seen in small ways. One fitting example is handling a customer's problem even when it does not directly relate to the company's product. When a customer is done transacting business with Dell, he or she has a sense of well-being and a friend at court in times of difficulty. It can be argued that, from the point of view of a Dell customer, he or she has bought service as much as a product.

---

minimal advertising, and depending largely on location and word-of-mouth conveyance to bring in new business. Business is retained by these firms solely on the basis of customer satisfaction and the consumer's returning for further purchases of the same services.

Marketing is vital to the stability and growth of service providers both because the benefit of the service is so intangible and because that benefit may be delayed as well. Take the category of advice giving. Many times, a substantial period of time must elapse before the full benefits to the consumer are fully realized.

Service Differentiation

Service marketers have a difficult time differentiating their service from their competitors'. To the consumer, law firms look a lot alike. The marketer must deal with this consumer dilemma. Price is a strong determinant with some buyers. Price may appear to be a proper distinction between two providers, but if this is so then the consumer must be led to understand that such a determination presumes that all other bases of comparison are essentially the same. Only then is price the main differentiator.

Yet dependency on price can be a trap. The attainments and market position of United Parcel Service are built not on price per se, but on consistency, dependability, and the predictability of its service. In this case, quality of service as perceived by the consumer is a major differentiation factor.

If one is purchasing health services and the providers competing with each other are a private physician, a walk-in medical service, and the emergency room of a hospital, then price may be a factor, as is speed of service delivery (expressed in waiting time). Of course, the quality of the service is also ultimately seen as a major factor. Let us remember that the full benefits of the service are often delayed. Foremost in the mind of the consumer may be the friendliness and empathy expressed by the employees they have direct contact with, as well as the quality and responsiveness of the physician's services.

The consumer's perception and expectation of each of the providers are also variables. In fact, the buying decision may be made on a comfort level, such as the nonthreatening aspect of the provider, the personalization of the service by the provider, or the speed of delivery. Certainly the demeanor of the people and general environment in the provider's establishment are major factors for many consumers. The "bedside manner" attributed to a physician by the patient may actually be the reason the service is purchased.

The marketer who ignores these many factors does so perilously. Management must perceive its operation through the eyes of its consumers and not prejudge those factors that will be of appeal.

Factors that can be developed to measure service quality are:

- Access—the service is easy to obtain in convenient locations
- Communication—the service is described accurately in the consumer's language
- Competence—the employees possess the required skill and knowledge
- Courtesy—the company and employees are respectful, friendly, and considerate
- Credibility—the company and employees are trustworthy and have the customer's best interests at heart
- Reliability—the service is performed with consistency and accuracy
- Responsiveness—the employees respond quickly and creatively to the customer's requests and problems
- Security—the service is free from danger, risk, or doubt
- Tangibles—the tangibles of the service correctly project the quality of the service
- Understanding or knowing the customer—the employees make an effort to understand the customer's needs and provide individual attention[2]

[2]A. Parasuraman, Valarie Zeithamel, and Leonard Berry, "A Conceptual Model of Service Quality and Its Implications for Future Research," *Journal of Marketing* (Fall 1985).

What Do Service Customers Want?

A recent U.S. Consumer Affairs study revealed that consumers frequently don't complain because they think it will do no good.

When it comes to service, customers care most about reliability, responsiveness, and empathy. Of these, reliability is critical. It is usually perceived as the weakest element of most companies' performance—and the greatest source of service problems. Service programs should provide all three elements. The net result will be satisfied customers, who are the key to long-term consumer loyalty.

• *Reliability*. This means promising only what you can deliver. If you perform what you've promised dependably, accurately, and consistently, customers will be confident you can do more. They will come back and bring new business with them.

• *Responsiveness*. If you respond swiftly to customers' problems, you will make them feel important. This, in turn, helps create customer confidence in the company. To ensure problems are dealt with promptly, employees should not only be courteous, but also up-to-date on the full range of products and services the company offers.

• *Empathy*. Customers want caring, individualized attention. They want to feel that theirs is a special case. Employees should be attentive, sympathetic and understanding of their needs and complaints. Customers' questions should be answered even if they are not directly related to a product or service you provide. Employees should be ready to present alternative solutions to customers in case the company is not able to help them.

Source: © 1990 ADWEEK. Used by permission of ADWEEK's Marketing Week.

Motivating employees to provide more and better service to the customer ensures that the customer will return to the company for additional purchases. Raising the level of sensitivity to the customer's needs, concerns, and fears is a means of raising the level of productivity of the organization. Losing the

Marketing for Nonprofit Organizations

The poorly conceived term *nonprofit* is often misunderstood by the general public. The public fails to understand that these organizations are usually forced to be just as rigorous about their business affairs as any for-profit company. This being the case, marketing the services of the organization and maximizing potential and market penetration are paramount goals.

Nonprofits have an equal need to broadcast their offerings to as wide a market as possible. All of the steps suggested in this book relating to organizing the marketing function and determining the customer profile in a for-profit business apply.

Frank W. Wylie, of California State University at Long Beach, says: "Marketing, a word once never heard in the health services field, is now the number one buzzword. Marketing presents the sensible alternative, the most plausible of the solutions [to slow growth in the economy]."

According to Wylie, marketing forces nonprofits to focus on what they're all about, determine their specific needs, and decide which groups and persons can help them to achieve their goals.

"It means we substitute research for guessing, and that we pay attention to what the research tells us," he says. "It means that we learn to plan ahead effectively, dealing with the realities rather than favoring traditional preferences.

"It means that marketing communication must become an integral part of the research, planning, execution, and evaluation of every activity."

Source: Karen Schwartz, "Nonprofits' Bottom-line," *Marketing News* (February 13, 1989), published by the American Marketing Association.

customer to a competitor because of indifference, inattention, or sloppy work is the worst thing that can happen to a service establishment. Particularly so, if this occurs in the face of having provided top-flight quality in competitive service.

Price is often a determinant in selecting a service provider. This is in large part because it is difficult for a customer to differentiate on any other basis. Judging a service establishment on price alone demeans the quality and the care that the provider offers in addition to the service itself. Customers will pay a higher price if they feel there is additional benefit to be gained. In the 1990s, service providers will succeed or fail on the basis of these added values.

An Example of Service Differentiation

Many neighborhoods have a dry cleaning establishment that competes on a basis other than price. It differentiates itself by offering special service for wedding and evening gowns, suede and leather cleaning, or summer storage of wool garments. Or it may compete on the ostensible basis of a higher-quality offering, using such terms as "French cleaning" to describe its process and charging a measurably higher price for its service. The marketing point to be seen here is the justification of higher price on the basis of higher quality offered, and some measure of additional service being provided.

The marketing of a service requires an intense focus on customer needs and wants. Knowledge of customers' comfort zones, that is, what they truly want from the service provider in addition to the service itself, is critical in the maintenance and growth of a service business. Since services are defined as intangible, the benefits may need to be renewed again and again. To most service businesses, repeat visits by the customer are the essence of growth.

Unfortunately, consumers' memories are very long when they have been disappointed. Restaurants that disappoint in service or product on a single occasion may suffer indefinitely, with that customer being unwilling to chance a repeat of the episode.

This tells us, then, that the key words in a service business are quality and consistency. It becomes management's primary task to maintain an unremitting focus on consistently delivering quality service responsive to customers' needs. Repeat visits and the benefits of word-of-mouth recommendations of satisfied customers to their friends and associates are the bases on which successful service businesses are built.

Management must set up close monitoring procedures for constant evaluation of the quality being delivered because of the dire and long-lived effects of quality slippage.

Customer Service or Lip Service?

In a recent survey by The Forum Corp., an international training and consulting firm based in Boston, 86 percent of 611 Fortune 500 executives polled named "quality of customer service" as "extremely important" to their company and a higher priority than ten other items, including productivity and company reputation. That's up from 68 percent who cited customer service as "extremely important" in 1986, Forum says.

The reason for the new emphasis is simple: Companies increasingly are finding that bad service costs customers. Seven of ten customers who switch from one company to a competitor cite poor service—not price or quality—as the reason, Forum surveys found. Good service, on the other hand, boosts revenue.

17

Managing the Product System

The combination of major product responsibilities with the sales, promotion, and related persuasion activities of a business is one of the fundamental characteristics of the marketing concept. Without substantial influence and authority wielded by the marketing department to help determine what products and services are offered and how they are to be priced, packaged, and distributed, we have a business that is in a state of avoidance of the marketing concept.

Product planning has to be a consumer-oriented activity for the company to compete effectively in chosen business arenas. What is required is consistent and perceptive listening to customers, dedicated attention to the ideas of the sales and distribution organizations, and persistent monitoring of the marketplace to keep abreast of what the competition may be expected to do next.

Where the marketing organization does not have this kind of involvement in managing the product system, the business is, at best, operating under a sales concept and with a sales orientation.

The Purpose of the Product System

The purpose of the product system is to ensure that you have the right product, at the right time, in the right place, at the right price to meet your customers' requirements.

Overall, the entire business and each of its segments can be considered a product system. We intend here to take a look at marketing's role in the overall product system and to examine the major relationships involved with other functions.

Different functions view the product in a different light. Note the typical responses of various functions to the question "What is the perfect product?"

- Sales: highest quality; lowest price; always in stock; unique features; unlimited models, sizes, and colors
- Engineering and Design: tough technical challenge; requires computer-assisted design; no drafting involved; complete design freedom; time and money needs fulfilled; a technical-journal article resulting
- Accounting and Finance: generates above-average profit; little investment required; no surprises; totally predictable sales and cash flow
- Production: same quantity every week; quality standards easy to meet; requires new plant and total retooling; will lead to total automation

To talk of a product *system* is not to suggest a highly technical approach, but rather to emphasize the need for an orderly, logical, and planned methodology to determine what to offer, when to present it, and how to make it available to customers.

Product System Methods

The product system can be viewed through the methods it employs to achieve a marketing orientation for the business:

- Product planning based on evaluation of customer needs
- Recommendations for new products based on market requirements and customer specifications for products
- Business objectives implemented through product line offerings

- Market testing to determine acceptance, preference, and demand
- Pricing, packaging, and branding for competitive advantage
- Production scheduled to meet customer, sales, and competitive requirements

The marketing department will provide leadership in the product planning system. This demands planning, programming, and implementation in a creative and continuous manner. It also requires the use of persuasion, and even aggressive methods, to ensure participation and contribution from the other functions in the business. Sharing the marketing point of view with others will help orient them to the marketplace.

It would be naïve to think that without this marketing activity the technical side of the company spontaneously delivers new product that suits customer requirements, or that production delivers it when the customer needs it. It is at least unlikely that the financial side reorients budgets and forecasts to meet unexpected change without marketing input. This influence from marketing helps keep the customer focus shared by the entire organization.

Product System Tools

Another way to view this is through analysis of the tools used to establish and operate an effective system:

- Research, including commercial intelligence and marketing research
- Product and market-segment analysis and definition
- Identifying sales, promotion, distribution, and service considerations that could impact product development
- Formulating marketing strategies for each segment
- Analyzing competitive offerings
- Assuring integration of all functions of the business on product teams

- Constant monitoring of the marketplace to measure customer acceptance and competitive standing and trends

Planning for Existing Product Lines

Much has been written about planning new products, but very little about the less glamorous work of product planning required for existing product lines. The list of activities presented here outlines the essential work for most businesses. The elements are shown in three categories, because there are distinct differences in requirements for each.

Administration of Current Line

- Identify needs, and plan for modifications of the product to expand the market.
- Determine appearance changes to meet annual model requirements.
- Change marketing specifications to permit cost improvements.
- Develop market specifications for line simplification, standardization, product structuring, and similar changes.
- Make decisions on special models, modifications from standard offerings, and other possible deviations for limited markets.

Advance Work

- Anticipate, interpret, and communicate customer requirement changes.
- Identify technical and production developments and trends, and evaluate their effect on existing product lines.
- Gather ideas for redesigning existing lines and for innovating new ones.
- Develop timely changes in business and marketing objectives and strategies.

Major Product Redesigns

- Develop proposals for increasing value by adding features, quality, performance, or other factors.
- Recommend changes to help to segment markets through product differentiation.
- Suggest means to give products competitive advantage.
- Participate with other functions in cost-reduction programs.

Product Elimination

One of the most troublesome and difficult tasks in managing the product system is the elimination of products that have outlived their usefulness. There may be many reasons for reluctance to do so:

Sentiment and nostalgia
Habit and resistance to change
Fear in the form of lost volume
Impact on fixed expenses
Lack of experience in leaving a business
A need for evaluation and decision tools

The most useful tool for making these decisions is a set of pruning criteria, such as the following six:

1. Profitability
   - What is the profit forecast for the current year?
   - What is the profit history for the last three, five, ten years?
   - What is the profit forecast for the next three to five years?
   These should be measured on such bases as percent of profit to sales, return on investment, residual income, cash flow, or other bases established in the company and its industry.

2. Growth-curve position
   - Is this a growing, static, or declining market? Apply this to each product line or market segment.
   - Are there opportunities for expanding the market?
3. Product leadership
   - How do products stand competitively in acceptance, preference, or demand?
   - What are the ratings of performance, attractiveness, and other customer considerations?
   - Analyze these by end-customer class, distribution channel, and any other buying influences.
4. Market leadership
   - What is the market share over the last five years?
   - Are there unserved or underserved market opportunities?
   - What are anticipated market-position trends?
   - Are there anticipated changes of a technical or production nature that would improve or threaten market position?
   - What is the current reading of and trend for competitive alignment?
5. Interdependence considerations
   - Does elimination have a negative effect on combined orders with other products?
   - What effect is there on the sales force, distributors, dealers, and agents?
   - What impact is there on the technical, production, and marketing functions? Does this limit their ability to serve customers effectively?
   - What impact is there on the technical, production, and marketing functions? Does this limit their ability to serve customers effectively?
   - What competitiveness effects are there on others of the company's lines?
6. Risks of elimination
   - What is the impact on the entire company?
   - Do supplier relationships suffer?
   - How does change affect public relations considerations regarding labor and community relations?

Product Planning Redefined

In many businesses, the product system suffers because of confusion about the respective roles of the various functions. There is also sometimes a problem of definition. One solution is to use the term *product planning* to describe the total task of determining what is offered for sale, with participation by all the relevant functions in the business.

Here are some of the questions that product planners attempt to answer:

- What are the market and business segments to be selected?
- Which customer classes, types of distribution, and competitive arenas should the business choose?
- What product lines, including models, styles, sizes, grades, shapes, and colors, should be offered?
- What are the customer requirements and market specifications for each item?
- Which customer or distributor requests for modifications are to be met?
- Should the line be full or limited?
- Should the business be a technical leader or follower?
- What kind of production capability and other resources are needed?
- What costs and other financial considerations arise?

These are only some examples of the range and variety of questions to which marketing must respond. Appropriate and continuous product planning will help to provide the answers.

Organizing for Product Planning

We are dealing with managing an effective product system through establishing and staffing the product-planning organization. A logical starting point is to identify its scope. This includes new products, existing products, and elimination of products. The functional inventory includes these activities:

- Commercial intelligence—collecting information on customer needs, benefits sought, buying behavior, and any related matters
- Objectives and strategies—formulating these as part of the overall outlook of the company
- Product ideas—gathering and processing ideas from within and outside the company
- Product specifications—interpreting customer requirements to the technical and production organizations in operational terms
- Product timing—establishing schedules for product introduction and product changes, communicating them throughout the organization, and monitoring implementation
- Product identification—developing brand recommendations, including selection of trademarks, names, packaging, and labeling

---

The Wall Street Journal quotes John Lister, of Lister Butler, a New York consulting firm, as saying: "Packaging is the last five seconds of marketing."

Companies are finding that it is a manageable alternative to an expensive national promotional and ad campaign and often more cost-benefit efficient.

The dilution of advertising effectiveness and penetration because of the battle for consumer attention among the many television channels and the number of new magazines has given packaging a new dimension of importance.

It has become that much more important to have your product stand out on the store shelf amid all of the clutter of competing brands seen in today's stores. The last thing that the buyer sees, the last penetrating image and recollection of the product, is in the packaging.

18

Managing the Persuasion System

Some of you may think that our plants and products are the most important assets of our business. As essential as they are, I don't agree with that. We could replace them pretty quickly. I'm convinced that two other, but less tangible, assets are the keys to our success. These are, first, our sales organization, which we must never forget nor neglect. Second is our advertising, promotion, and merchandising competence. With the latter, we build customer demand, preference, and acceptance.

The speaker is the corporate marketing director of one of the largest industrial-products companies in the United States.

The approach this company takes is to build a persuasion system that communicates with and influences customers continually and powerfully. This man keeps in his office a poster: "Don't confuse the customer." He sees such an error as a cardinal sin.

He understands that logical and integrated use of many persuasion tools and methods is what it takes to expand markets and obtain orders in a competitive setting. He reviews his sales organization's activities and distribution mechanisms, and he makes constant customer contacts himself to ensure that every aspect of persuasion for influencing customers is in operation at peak efficiency.

Purpose of the Persuasion System

The purpose of the persuasion system is disarmingly simple to state, but frustratingly difficult to achieve: to get orders through market development and customer cultivation. This involves getting the right information with the right appeal to the right customer at the right time in the right manner. We can see the entire marketing operation, including the product and support system, as a total persuasion system. For this purpose, the scope of the persuasion system includes sales and distribution, advertising and promotion, market development, merchandising, customer assistance and education, and related activities.

The term *system* as used here is not intended to suggest a highly technical approach, but simply to emphasize the need for an orderly, logical, and planned methodology in taking products to market and convincing customers to buy them.

The Persuasion Planning Process

Remember that in a marketing-oriented approach to the marketplace, we want to review the inputs, activities, and outputs of persuasion planning.

Inputs include intelligence about:

- Customers
- Markets
- Competition
- The business environment

Activities may be summarized as:

- Identifying and evaluating market opportunities
- Formulating persuasion objectives and strategies
- Commmunicating courses of action, by the persuasion group
- Reconciling persuasion plans with product/support plans
- Defining persuasion approaches to be used

Outputs of persuasion planning are:

- Courses of actions to be followed, including objectives, strategies, schedules, and assignments
- Definition of persuasion approaches for each market segment and for the business as a whole
- Sales, promotion, merchandising, advertising, and other persuasion programs
- Recommendations from a persuasion point of view to guide product and support-system planning

Planning emphasis should be on formulating persuasion objectives and strategies that are derived from the overall business and marketing objectives.

The preferred method for defining precise objectives is a critical phase of persuasion planning. The range of goals runs the gamut from closing immediate sales through building long-term consumer franchises and establishing brand-name and company image.[1]

Organizing the Persuasion System

A useful starting point in organizing the persuasion system in any business is to define the critical problems to be resolved.

- What work should be done within the company, and what should be done outside by distributors, advertising agencies, and other suppliers?
- What work should be done at headquarters, and what should be done in the field?
- How can we effectively integrate advertising, sales promotion, and sales training with sales activities?

[1]Many years ago, management consultant Russell H. Colley developed an advertising checklist covering fifty-two areas of tasks, replete with examples and applications. It is as fresh and applicable today as it was when developed over thirty years ago. See Russell H. Colley, *Defining Advertising Goals for Measured Advertising Results* (New York: Association of National Advertisers, 1961).

- Should the structure be based primarily on products, markets, or other considerations?
- How can we provide balanced attention for planning and implementing activities?

Here is a definition of the total work to be done in order to allocate resources appropriately. A comprehensive inventory includes the following activities:

- *Commercial intelligence.* Collect information about customers, markets, distribution, competition, and the business environment. Process and utilize the results for persuasion planning and implementation.
- *Persuasion planning.* Formulate persuasion objectives and strategies in concert with overall business and marketing objectives and strategies. Develop and communicate courses of action for sales, distribution, advertising, sales promotion, and merchandising programs.
- *Persuasion approaches.* Develop approaches for taking products and services to market, including appropriate sales and distribution channels.
- *Market development.* Formulate programs for expanding existing markets through the persuasion approach.
- *Sales administration.* Establish and manage suitable administrative and control procedures for the operation of sales and distribution. Included will be quotations, propositions, requisitions, and other systematic approaches. Coordinate with sales support and all other functions of the business.
- *Sales services.* Establish sales-engineering and customer-education programs along with any other sales services needed. Coordinate these with sales support and the other business functions.
- *Advertising administration.* Establish suitable administrative and control procedures for effective operation of advertising, sales promotion, publicity, merchandising, and other communications activities. Direct and coordinate the advertising-agency relationship. Provide communications services to the other business functions.

Ten Criteria for Successful Ads

1. *High degree of visual magnetism.* Must stop the reader's eye while scanning the pages.

2. *Selects the right audience.* Must relate to the reader's problems or opportunities.

3. *Invites the reader into the scene.* Illustrative material must relate to the reader's interests and background.

4. *Promises a reward.* The reader must foresee that something of value will be attained.

5. *Backs up the promise.* Hard evidence is presented that the reward promised is valid and attainable.

6. *Presents the selling proposition in logical sequence.* Guides the reader through the ad in the proper order of the development of the idea.

7. *Talks person-to-person.* Speaks as one friend telling another friend about a good deal.

8. *Is easy to read.* Type choice and layout are vital in stopping and holding the reader.

9. *Emphasizes the service, not the source.* The reader must be convinced, first, *to buy* before *where* to buy.

10. *Reflects the company's character.* The things that will make the company liked, respected, and admired; closely portrays the company's personality.

Source: "The Copy Chasers," *Business Marketing* (January 1992).

• *Selling and customer relations.* Establish and maintain contacts and relationships with customers and prospects.

• *Persuasion personnel.* Provide for recruiting, selection, placement, training and development, motivation, compensation, and performance evaluation for all persuasion personnel.

Having delineated the tasks of the persuasion system, we now turn to developing a suitable organizational structure for accomplishing the required work. Here are some basic alternatives:

• *Product line.* When the business includes diverse lines

with little in common, it is often advisable to provide persuasion units dedicated to each line. This may embrace sales, advertising, and promotion. This type of activity can be combined with product planning and placed under individual product managers.

• *Brand.* When competing brands are involved, separate provision is usually advisable for each. The functions of persuasion, product planning, and other related activities can be combined under separate brand managers.

• *Individual functions.* When several similar product lines or salable services are involved, or when specialization is important, a functional organization of persuasion activities may be appropriate. For example, separate units may be established for sales, advertising, market development, and other persuasion functions.

• *New versus old products.* When specialized effort is required for market development, for introducing new markets, or for other long-range purposes, separate units may be advisable.

• *Market or industries.* When distinct market characteristics such as application or system requirements are a predominant consideration, separate organization units may be desirable for each market served. In some cases like this, product and persuasion activities may be combined to provide concentration.

• *Project, system, or order.* This organization is important when the business is highly technical. In this situation, product planning and other marketing functions can also be combined.

• *Customer.* This approach is used when you are a supplier of components or resources to an end-product manufacturer. You then create an operation to service that customer, probably integrating product planning and production scheduling with the persuasion areas.

• *Distribution channel.* When the distribution channel is a critical consideration, separate persuasion operations may be desirable. Particularly when product requirements vary by channel, it may be desirable to combine persuasion, product planning, production scheduling, and other relevant functions into a channel-focused unit of the marketing organization.

• *Geography.* When territorial characteristics vary substantially, some form of regional organization may best suit customer requirements. Be certain to designate which activities will be performed at headquarters and which ones will be done in the region.

To avoid any confusion of responsibility, it is important to delineate responsibilities clearly among distributors, advertising agencies, public relations agencies, and other parties in the persuasion process.

The persuasion function is unusually vulnerable to shifts in market conditions. When the economic situation wavers and volume dips, sales and promotion budgets are often a target for pruning. Accordingly, it is important to provide for flexibility to adapt to change. One way to do this is to evaluate suitability of staffing for the anticipated level of volume, that is, for a drop or rise of 25 percent.

Selecting Approaches for Persuasion

We discussed selection of approaches briefly in Chapter 12 as a consideration in defining business and market segments. Here we are dealing with analyzing and selecting persuasion approaches as an element in managing the persuasion system.

We want an orderly approach to determine how products and services are taken to market. As in all systems analysis, this involves classifying activities, arranging them in suitable patterns, identifying and evaluating alternatives, and selecting an appropriate approach for each situation.

When persuasion approaches are based on past practices, industry custom, or the whims of management, generalized approaches can result that are often suitable for one segment of the business but illogically extended to all others.

A persuasion approach is defined as the basic method employed to reach customers having common requirements in a given business arena. This approach is determined by:

- Customer classification
- Type of purchase
- Nature of product or service offering
- Sales and distribution channel employed

These characteristics can vary greatly for different segments of a single product line.

A convenient starting point for defining the persuasion approach is to consider each of the four elements of a persuasion approach while analyzing each market segment.

1. *Customer classification.* Emphasis here is on the end customer. Some of the categories are:

- Consumer end user
- Commercial end user
- Institutional end user
- Industrial end user
- Original equipment manufacturer
- Government, for civilian use
- Government, for defense use

Here we are providing for differences in needs, in benefits and advantages sought, and in end-use characteristics. For example, separate categories would be required for consumer markets to distinguish home consumers of packaged products from users of home supplies or home services.

2. *Type of purchase.* The search is for patterns of buying. While the categories may vary by type of business, this grouping shows some of the more common types of purchase:

- Frequent repeat purchase
- Frequent impulse purchase
- One-time purchase
- Periodic or continuous supply
- Contracts
- Sealed bids
- Packaged orders with other items

For example, in a consumer market you could segregate by repeat, impulse, and considered purchase.

A municipal equipment market could break down to annual supply contracts, sealed bid projects, and no-bid buys.

3. *Product or service.* Patterns in this element will be derived from the product or service itself:

- Packaged product for home consumption
- Housewares device for home use
- Major appliance for home use
- Equipment for commercial use
- Commercial supplies
- Commercial products for resale
- Industrial plant equipment
- Components for original equipment
- Replacement parts and supplies
- Industrial plant service

For example, consumer products would have separate classifications for packaged offerings, devices for home use, and major appliances.

4. *Sales and distribution channels.* This analysis considers:

- Direct sale—specialized sales force
- Direct sale—general sales force
- Company-owned distribution
- Independent distributors and dealers, manufacturers' agents
- Wholesalers and jobbers
- Contractors

Distinctions include market coverage, form and frequency of sales contact, and technical or educational requirements. For example, utility or defense markets usually call for direct sales contact. Industrial-components customers commonly require specialized sales contact. Consumer-housewares buyers utilize retail distribution coverage.

Having completed these four analyses, persuasion planners should develop a classification of persuasion approaches to accommodate all of the customer classes, types of purchases, product and service offerings, and sales and distribution channels appropriate to the business. Spreadsheets like that in Table 3 are useful for this purpose.

As an example of using the spreadsheet, a furniture manufacturer might have its own retail outlets in selected metropolitan markets, its own wholesale distribution house in secondary markets, and independent wholesalers covering still other markets. In such a case, each of the three is classified as a distinct persuasion approach.

Recognize that where promotional, educational, or technical assistance is a consideration, further refinement may be called for.

The following are some of the activities in which clearly defined persuasion approaches are useful.

• *Organization.* All product-marketing situations utilizing a consumer resale-consumption approach might be segregated from those using a consumer resale-use approach or a commercial-supply approach, where type of purchase, customer information, and influence warrant.

• *Distribution.* Decisions about whether to employ a direct-customer or an indirect-distribution channel, and whether to provide specialized or generalized sales assignments are influenced by such considerations as effective coverage and impact in all markets served.

For example, an industrial business may find that use of an industrial-installation approach employing contractors for certain product lines and an industrial repeat-equipment approach may best be handled by manufacturer's agents.

• *Sales forces.* Each persuasion approach requires different types, numbers, and arrangements of sales forces. For example, in original-equipment markets, a direct consumer-product/ OEM approach with highly qualified sales engineers may be used for a few major customers among appliance manufacturers. On the other hand, a producer-goods/OEM approach is

Table 3. Examples of persuasion approaches.

Customer classification	Type of purchase	Product or service offering
Consumer end user	Frequent repeat purchase	Packaged product for home consumption
Consumer end user	Infrequent impulse purchase	Housewares device for home use
Consumer end user	One-time purchase	Major appliance or home equipment
Commercial or institutional end user	Frequent repeat purchase	Supplies or replacement parts
Commercial or institutional end user	Infrequent repeat purchase	Equipment for operation of facility
Commercial or institutional end user	One-time purchase	Major equipment for operation of facility
Commercial	Periodic or continuous supply	Products for resale
Commercial	Periodic or occasional purchase	Service for operating or maintaining facility
Industrial end user	Frequent repeat purchase	Supplies or replacement parts
Industrial end user	Infrequent repeat purchase	Plant equipment
Industrial end user	One-time purchase	Major installation plant equipment
Original-equipment manufacturer	Frequent repeat purchase	Materials for use in consumer products
Original-equipment manufacturer	Periodic or occasional purchase	Components for use in producer end products
Government, for defense	Contracts and projects	End-use products, components, and services

Sales and distribution channels employed	Examples of users	Persuasion-approach classification
Two-stage distributor and retail dealer	Food, drug, soap manufacturers	Consumer resale consumption
Two-stage distributor and retail dealer	Small appliance, dish, toy manufacturers	Consumer resale use
Manufacturer to retailer	Major appliance, furniture manufacturers	Consumer resale equipment
Direct, one-, or two-stage	Stationery, soap manufacturers	Commercial supply
Direct, agent, or distributor	Office, restaurant equipment manufacturers	Commercial equipment
Direct, contractor, or manufacturers' agent	Hotel, hospital equipment manufacturers	Commercial installation
Direct, agent, or distributor	Food, camera, notion manufacturers	Commercial resale
Direct	Cleaning or maintenance suppliers	Commercial service
Direct, distributor, jobber, or agent	Lubricant, wiring-device producers	Industrial supply
Direct, distributors, agents, contractors	Electric-motor and control manufacturers	Industrial repeat equipment
Direct, contractors	Turbine, machine-tool manufacturers	Industrial installation
Direct, manufacturers' agent	Steel mills, chemical producers	Consumer-product, original-equipment manufacturer
Direct, manufacturers' agent	Gasoline-engine, compressor manufacturers	Producer-goods, original-equipment manufacturer
Direct, government contractor	Jet-engine, computer manufacturers	Government, for defense

employed with manufacturer's agents covering diverse or scattered markets.

Promotion. Each persuasion approach presents unique opportunities and problems for utilizing different types and amounts of advertising, sales promotion, and merchandising effort.

For example, an industrial-installation or government-defense approach might emphasize prestige advedrtising, and even individual customer campaigns when major contracts are at stake. By contrast, an industrial-supply approach may emphasize trade-paper or direct-mail advertising where related products are offered to a large number of scattered customers.

Operating the Persuasion System

The marketing vice-president of one of the nation's largest diversified companies became concerned about maintaining the proper balance between his planning activities and his implementing tasks. He made a thorough time study of his allocations and found that he was not allocating time as he thought he was. Further, he found the same was true of his delegating.

When this executive retired, the president of the company used this time study as a guide in assigning responsibilities and in selecting a successor to the marketing person.

One useful way to maintain a balanced perspective is to maintain a marketing-oriented approach to the competitive arena. This calls upon marketing management to provide leadership in all aspects of the persuasive process. The approach demands continuous, creative, and innovative planning and implementation within the company. But it helps ensure that the technical functions direct their efforts to the realities and demands of the marketplace. This means getting design engineers and researchers out into the field to meet customers and acquaint themselves with customer needs and desires. It includes use of production and purchasing personnel to assist in persuasion activities, including field visits and even factory visits by customers.

The purchasing director of a major company points out

that they send teams to visit suppliers to evaluate their technical and production facilities. If they find a customer-oriented philosophy there, the chances improve measurably that their own company is being served effectively.

While most businesses give concentrated attention to precisely defining sales territories and monitoring distribution arrangements, media decisions, and such aspects of persuasion management, there is an even more fundamental evaluation of resource allocation that does not always get adequate attention. This involves questions relating to:

- Direct sales force versus indirect distribution
- Sales effort versus promotional activities
- Broad versus selective sales and distribution coverage
- Basic media selection among advertising, sales promotion, direct mail, audiovisual, special promotions, and many additional alternatives

Too often, these decisions are made by whim, by dint of special pleading, or by management habit. Sometimes they are even made by the dictates of the budgeting bias of the accounting department.

Astute marketing management assures that these decisions are made through a formal analytical process that considers:

- Market opportunities and alternatives
- Media appropriateness for each market segment
- Leverage of the various persuasion tools

This should result in tailoring decisions to accomplish specific marketing objectives and strategies.

Successful Persuasion Examples

The marketing director of a consumer-appliance business emphasizes the importance of being consumer-oriented in the distribution process. Her advice is to continually modify and tailor

Positioning Defined

Positioning starts with a product, a piece of merchandise, a service, a company, an institution, or even a person.

But positioning is not what you do to a product. Positioning is what you do to the mind of the prospect. That is, you position the product in the mind of the prospect.

So it's incorrect to call the concept "product positioning." You're not really doing something to the product itself.

Not that positioning doesn't involve change. It often does. But changes made in the name, the price, and the package are really not changes in the product at all. They're basically cosmetic changes done for the purpose of securing a worthwhile position in the prospect's mind.

approaches, channels, and persuasion approaches to changing markets and consumer desires, tastes, habits, and even whims.

David Merrick, the famous Broadway producer, once expressed his attitude toward his customers. He decided that a play in an out-of-town tryout stage just was not up to his standards and reputation. He canceled the New York opening, refunded $1.5 million in advance ticket sales, and, with his backers, took that loss. He reasoned that his customer base, knowing why he had done so, would continue unhesitatingly to buy advance tickets for Merrick productions in the future.

The top marketing executive of a leading packaged-food company strongly emphasizes the selling process. He promotes a continuous sales effort around the values of the products. He asks for an old-fashioned, hard-sell approach to be certain that every customer is influenced about the values of the product line. His own organization reflects this in its every contact with customers, from the lowest-ranked job function up through the general manager.

The marketing manager of a diversified industrial company sees the sales engineer as the key persuasion agent of the company. This person's role is both as the company's voice with customers and as the communicator of the customer point of view back to the company. In order to motivate customers to purchase the company's products, someone has to understand and communicate the customer's real needs back to the company. The sales process does not simply offer a product; rather, it makes a genuine contribution to solving the customer's problems through the purchase of the company's product. The sales person integrates all of the company's efforts and resources toward fulfillment of the customer's needs.

19

Managing the Support System

It is important to ask the following questions about marketing support activity in your company:

1. Is this activity viewed as a cost or profit drain, or as a necessary nuisance?
2. Is it considered to be an obligation grudgingly met and invoked only when an explicit customer complaint is received?
3. Is it viewed as a positive and constructive contribution to selling more products or services?
4. Is it seen as a way of gaining and holding customer loyalty to your company because of the responsiveness of your marketing support services and attitudes?

Would your customers agree with your evaluation?

In this chapter, we look at some current examples of companies using positive, opportunity-focused approaches.

Dell Computers, an OEM in Austin, Texas, takes the approach that if their customer is having a problem with Dell equipment, the burden is transferred to Dell to help find a solution. In some cases, Dell has labored to correct a software or operating system problem for the customer even though it lies outside of Dell's purview, which is the hardware. Imagine how such an attitude bonds a customer to a supplier.

Many companies provide a toll-free 800 telephone number for customers to order products. But many fewer provide toll-free numbers for customer service or technical support. This implies a not-so-subtle distinction in corporate thinking, between fulfilling "my need versus your need."

We are not suggesting, even for a moment, acceding to irresponsible or frivolous customer demand. What is suggested is treating the customer as you expect to be treated by your suppliers. Further, we suggest striving to resolve any differences in a manner that tends toward full customer satisfaction. It is a truism of marketing that it is a lot harder and far more expensive to find and sell a new customer than it is to hold on to an existing one.

As a self-test of the responsiveness of your marketing support function, answer four questions:

1. Do you regularly review your activities so that changes in the marketplace, your product, pricing, or scheduling are reflected in your support attitudes and procedures?
2. Are your marketing support facilities located and managed as your customers need them to be?
3. Or are they managed according to the status quo or industry customs? Leadership positions are established through innovative thinking, not through slavishly following others' practices.
4. When you have a product failure, an inadequate complaint policy, or a safety disaster, do you react quickly with adjusted policies? Or do you adopt a bunker mentality, ducking out of the line of fire in the hope that it will all eventually die down?

Regular reading of the newspapers amply demonstrates practices worth emulating or avoiding.

A classic case may be how the McNeill Laboratories division of consumer-products giant Johnson & Johnson underwent a product-tampering situation. Public information was immediately disseminated; total openness and full disclosure was the approach taken. The company rode out a potential disaster with flying colors and no loss of public trust. It is important to remember that there was contingency planning in place *before* the event took place.

Compare this with the terrible disaster at the Chernobyl nuclear generation plant in the former Soviet Union. The approach taken was to withhold information on the nature and scope of the mishap for days. The public was denied its right to know and thereby was unable to take suitable action to protect itself and to minimize the health hazards.

Purpose of the Support System

The marketing manager of a business-equipment manufacturer looks to his support system for information and analyses that assist managing many aspects of his operation.

- How many of our customers contribute to profit?
- How many of our customers cost us real money?
- How much of this is in the nature of the customers?
- How much of this is due to our own nature?
- How many of our prospects can we convert to customers?
- What sales approach can accomplish this?
- Will any of these become unprofitable customers?
- How many sales calls are we making on potentially unprofitable prospects?
- What sales and sales-support patterns are most effective to open profitable accounts, hold profitable accounts, and regain lost profitable accounts?
- How effective is each of our sales managers and sales representatives?

This marketing executive maintains that an effective, well-managed support system provides answers to these questions.

In this sense, the term *support system* is not meant to define the technical, engineering, or scientific supports that some lines require. We are talking instead of an orderly customer-support system relating to our marketing approaches.

Organizing the Support System

A useful starting point for organizing the support system is recognition of the type of critical problems to be resolved. While there is variance depending on the type of business, these questions are usually of this order:

- What kinds of support work do we do inside? What is to be done outside by distributors or agents?
- Which support activities should be pooled, and which should be decentralized by product line, market, or channel?
- What work should be done at a single central point, at various plant locations, or in the field?
- How should support activities interface with engineering or production, where close teamwork is necessary?
- Should the support system be based primarily on products, markets, or other considerations?
- How should balanced attention be provided for planning and implementing activities of the support system?
- How should the support system be linked to intelligence gathering and other information sources essential for support planning and operation?

List of Support Activities

Possible support activities include:

- Intelligence gathering—collect information on customers, markets, distribution, competition, and the business environment
- Support planning—formulate support objectives and strategies for the overall marketing objectives; develop courses of action for specific programs
- Sales budgeting—develop and monitor sales budgets for each territory and the entire business
- Production scheduling—develop and operate a production scheduling system that reflects customer and distri-

bution needs; establish and maintain close teamwork relationships with the production organization

- Inventory control—develop and operate an inventory control system that is based on customer and distribution requirements, and integrated with the sales budget and production scheduling system
- Physical distribution—develop and operate a physical distribution system, including transportation, warehousing, and delivery, that is fully integrated with other systems
- Marketing-expense budgets—develop and monitor expense budgets that are oriented to marketing plans and are compatible with the accounting and control systems of the company
- Marketing records and statistics—arrange for the accounting organization to supply marketing records, statistics, and other essential data for effective management and control
- Product service—develop a product service system designed to satisfy customer expectations, including warranties, installation, parts supply, repairs, complaint handling, and related customer services
- Order servicing—establish and operate an order-entry program to accommodate the requirements of the several elements of the business
- Financial services—develop sales financing, credit and collection, and any other financial services required to serve customers effectively
- Marketing office management—provide facilities, office services, and other administrative assistance required for efficient and economical operation of the marketing function

Reviews of these services should be held with the other functions of the company, either providing some of these services or being informed by them to be certain that there are no misunderstandings or conflicts.

The actual final organization of this support function is determined by the structure the marketing organization takes.

The listings given here should be seen as checklists of functions and services, not as directive or organizational in their intent.

Operating the Support System

Our purpose is to consider, from the viewpoint of the marketing manager, some of the activities, decision areas, and relationships involved in managing the support system. The emphasis is on the kinds of services provided, competitive considerations, investment requirements, and the impact on profitability.

- Should we seek to make the customer self-sufficient, or dependent upon us? What services in each scenario should we be offering?
- Should our services emphasize quality, speed, and convenience? Or should we offer efficiency, economy, and low cost?
- Should we respond only to customer needs and expectations, or should we take the initiative in providing services and in raising the customer's expectations of us?
- Should we simply meet moral and legal obligations and the reasonable expectations of our customers, or should we attempt to differentiate our service offerings from those of competitors who may be doing only that?
- How do we presently compare to competitors in our support activities? Are we superior, equal, or inferior?
- In such areas as service and credit, should we attempt to make a profit, or include these services in the value of the total offering?
- Are we achieving a proper balance between provision of a level of customer service required by the marketing orientation of the business and, on the other hand, the operating requirements of cost control, efficiency, and direct contribution to profitability?

Unless the marketing people keep asking these questions periodically, then customer service and operating efficiency are likely to fail to keep up with changing marketplace requirements.

The key term is *consistency* in continual monitoring of all of the elements in the company that impact and contribute to providing support and customer services.

In monitoring services, analysis of the data and information provided by the management information systems people is mandatory.

We must constantly ask ourselves and our people: "How can we improve our service to customers?" The question should be asked of every function in the company, and certainly of every person in the marketing loop. This includes those inside and outside, and those who work for the company directly and indirectly (thereby taking in those who are distributors, agents, and subcontractors as well).

Let us not forget to have marketing executives make constant and consistent contact with customers and the marketplace. Whether this takes place at trade shows or in the field, the question is to be asked constantly and the answers carefully attended: "How can we better serve your needs?"

Only in this manner do we design, build, and maintain a sensitive support system for the company.

20

Selecting the Marketing Manager

In this chapter, we deal with the profile of a successful marketing manager. This is useful whether one is promoting from within or working with a recruitment firm to select the best candidate for this important role in a vital, dynamic organization.

What the Marketing Manager Needs to Be

If you study job descriptions developed by marketing-sophisticated companies and analyze work requirements, you will see what the marketing manager needs to be and the qualities he or she needs to have:

A business generalist. The ideal person is an entrepreneur who has good and refined business judgment, someone who has mastered the concept of risk/reward relationships and is a natural innovator. Since this person is a key member of the general management team, he or she has a well-rounded understanding and appreciation of the functions of finance, manufacturing, and design. This is important because of the necessity of integrating marketing with all of the other functions within the company.

A marketing specialist. Since this person is seen by the rest of the organization as the top marketing expert in the company, there should be a background in at least two of the principal marketing functions, preferably with sales or sales management as one of them. The marketing manager must have the communicative and persuasive abilities to represent marketing needs and goals to the rest of management.

A professional manner. The marketing manager must demonstrate the ability to manage the work, the people who are doing it, and the finances available to accomplish the goals of the marketing function. A planner, an organizer, an integrator, and an evaluator of the efforts of others: these are among the managerial talents needed. Innovativeness and skill at managing change are critical talents as well.

Leadership qualities. Look for soundness of character and the personality to sell his or her ideas, inspire action, and elicit cooperation. The combination of analytical and creative abilities needed to envision new approaches, consider alternatives, and evaluate courses of action is a key to fulfilling the management challenge.

In addition to these demanding qualifications, a feel for and understanding of the industry and the competitive arena are most important here.

What the Marketing Manager Must Know

The professional marketing manager must know the business in depth. A thorough understanding of each business segment, of their interrelationships, and of the business as a whole requires intimate knowledge of:

- Customers and markets
- Competition
- Sales, distribution, and service channels
- Products and services, as seen by customers
- The company and the industry
- The tools and methods of marketing
- Their relevance and application to the business

If this business is one in which technology is important, the marketing manager must be thoroughly acquainted with those aspects of research, engineering, and production that impact the company.

New and complex problems in marketing are dealt with by being familiar with information systems and the procedures of systems analysis and synthesis.

What the Marketing Manager Has to Do

Assuming that the marketing manager has these qualifications, what is to be done with them? While some industries are distinct in their special characteristics, there are five principal tasks common to every marketing management situation:

1. To develop, sponsor, and implement a marketing-oriented attitude and philosophy throughout the business
2. To build, foster, and maintain a customer-oriented marketing organization
3. To initiate and maintain a high level of market-focused strategic planning
4. To manage a dynamic marketing operating system that is effective, efficient, and economical

---

Alan G. Wernick, former vice president of personnel of Philip Morris Industrial, says: "Our standards and criteria for a director of marketing for one of our companies are to find a person who has familiarity with the marketplace and the product lines with which she or he would be involved.

"In addition, and sometimes overlooked, is the ability to interface well and communicate clearly with other managers and functions. We are not looking for a technician, we need a manager. Obviously, the ability to organize tasks and a department and to lead and motivate the people involved is a given."

Source: Interview with author.

5. To appraise and measure marketing performance with emphasis on maintaining balance between profit and growth objectives

High standards of ethics and performance, a sense of responsibility to the public, and a drive to lead by example rather than by mandate are also critical qualities to look for.

Part Five
Appraising Marketing Performance

21

A Marketing
Appraisal System

Too often, a profit or growth crisis, unusual competitive pressure, the threat of a takeover, a change in management staffing or personnel, or some other emergency is necessary before management calls for and conducts a full-blown appraisal of the effectiveness of its various functions.

Management needs to conceive, initiative, and maintain an orderly system and process for appraising performance for each segment and function of the business. A casual review of normal accounting reports and sales figures is not an adequate appraisal system. Appraisals after-the-fact must be superseded by evaluations that concentrate on anticipated results and that look to the future. Management needs measures that can be taken *before* crises occur.

Of course, any appraisal of the marketing function must be synchronous with appraisal of overall business performance. Unless this is done, one may be evaluating marketing in a vacuum, that is, ignoring the marketplace realities.

Purpose

An adequate appraisal of the business recognizes the three key elements of purpose in any business:

1. Survival
2. Growth
3. Profitability

Any appraisal system needs to be designed and tested to ensure that it accommodates these elements. It needs to evaluate the provisions for and obstacles to survival. It needs to evaluate plans and programs for both current and longer-range profitability, striving for balance between the two. And it needs to assess the compatibility of growth and profit objectives and strategies.

Appraisal Methods

To determine the method of appraisal to be used, consider these alternatives:

- Review performance against approved business plans
- Give attention to current problems, or exceptions to normal and expected performance
- Heed changes in external and internal factors and conditions

A common checklist used in business appraisal includes:

- Profitability
- Market position
- Product leadership
- Personnel development
- Employee attitudes
- Public responsibility
- Productivity
- Balance between short- and long-range goals

Evaluation Standards

In addition to those listed above, other appraisal alternatives are:

- Percentage of profit on sales
- Return on investment
- Inventory turnover
- Residual income
- Contributed value
- Profitability standards for individual segments, based on competitive arenas

Marketing performance is appraised in many different ways. Whether you are establishing an appraisal system or evaluating your present approach, these are some of the key considerations:

- Determining who makes the actual appraisal
- Choosing the method to be employed
- Selecting the appraisal categories
- Establishing the frequency of appraisals

Of course, any procedures, standards, or values you generally use in appraising the overall functioning of the business are appropriate for consideration in the marketing appraisal. It is strongly suggested that the accounting, finance, and marketing-information functions be consulted for advice and cooperation in making changes or improvements in the reporting processes, and for professional advice from those specialists.

1. *Who does the appraisal?* In many companies, direct-line management is held accountable for this appraisal process. In others, corporate staff or outside consultants are utilized. In decentralized operations, some form of self-appraisal is usually the most effective approach. However, a combination of these three approaches is often found to be the best. Utilizing consultants and nonmarketing people permits a more open, less turf-protecting attitude in the process. But exercise care to avoid undesirable duplication of effort or confusing conflict of authority.

2. *Choosing the method.* There are several basic ways to conduct the marketing appraisal. These include informal observation, reliance on financial reports, establishing and monitoring

productivity standards, and measuring the progress of implementation of approved plans. The decision is usually a matter of emphasis, combining several methods.

3. *Appraisal categories.* Among the ways of classifying marketing effort and performance are:

- Organization units
- Functions
- Markets served
- Product lines
- Territories
- Product acceptance
- Market development
- Distribution channels
- Marketing services
- Competitive ranking

4. *Frequency.* In some fast-moving businesses, such as chain and department stores and automobile dealerships, continuous or daily appraisals of results are common. Manufacturing businesses usually employ periodic appraisals, with frequency ranging from monthly through quarterly or annual.

Where management by exception is employed, frequency is usually determined by emergencies or unexpected events or problems. In such cases, accounting or other report systems may signal the need for an appraisal.

Seasonal businesses dictate their own appraisal frequency.

A Self-Appraisal Approach

The system proposed here is based on the assumption that the marketing function is operating under the marketing concept. It incorporates ideas and procedures gained through study of the appraisal literature and discussions with marketing and management consultants who specialize in evaluation work.

The key figure in this approach is the marketing manager. Selected members of the marketing staff—usually the heads of each department in the marketing function—conduct the appraisal. Other members of the organization are brought in as their contributions are needed. Outside consultants are brought in for advice and for substantive contributions where appropriate.

The underlying assumption is that self-appraisal has many advantages over appraisals by outsiders. We believe that the managers of the marketing operation are best qualified to evaluate their own performance, and that the action requirements flowing from the appraisal can be best met through a participative approach.

Essentially, the appraisal sessions are discussion meetings. A recorder is assigned to take notes on conclusions and on action plans developed. The agenda is built upon the appraisal categories selected.

Selecting Appraisal Categories

Many factors influence the choice of appraisal categories for a particular business:

- The nature of the product lines
- The markets served
- The distribution approach
- The existing organization and staffing
- The prevailing style of management

Since both sequence of coverage and selection of categories for review are vital to a successful appraisal process, the classification should be developed before the process is started. The team needs to be free, however, to modify the agenda as the process develops.

We propose ten appraisal categories that reflect the scope of marketing as we have developed it in this book:

1. Leadership in managing change
2. Marketing orientation
3. Marketing organization

4. Marketing personnel
5. Strategic planning
6. Product system
7. Pricing policy and practice
8. Persuasion system
9. Support system
10. Marketing results

Please note that all marketing activities fit into these categories. Appraisers need not be concerned when an activity appears in more than one category. Because different aspects and relationships are involved, there should be no concern about overlap or duplication.

Let us examine each appraisal category.

Leadership in Managing Change

This category provides perspective on the whole appraisal process. By focusing on future opportunities, the following questions encourage attention to modifications required to adapt to changing conditions in the marketplace.

• *Having a vision for the business.* Do we have a vision? What is it? Is it marketing-oriented? Is it understood and accepted by the organization? How should it be modified and improved?

• *Visualizing profit opportunities.* Is adequate attention given to future customer needs and wants? Have we proposed any major new ventures in the last two years? Can we identify any to be explored at this time? Can product lines, distribution schemes, or services be pruned to free up resources for other use? Are we providing guidance to the other company functions on market opportunities?

• *Taking calculated risks.* Are we missing opportunities for entering new businesses? Have we established goals with high reward potential?

• *Sponsoring innovation.* What is our record in innovating products and finding new applications? What new distribution patterns, persuasion approaches, or promotion appeals have we developed?

Discussions can identify subjects for further study within marketing and with other functions in the organization.

Marketing Orientation

The purpose here is to take stock of progress made in implementing the marketing concept as the basic attitude of the business. We may find that fundamental differences of opinion among staff members need to be resolved. Customer research may be required to resolve contradictory evaluations.

Questions arise in planning the offering:

- Do we visualize creatively how company capability can be used to serve our customers profitably?
- Are we able to say what we need to do, what it will take for us to win in the marketplace?
- What is our record in providing functional specifications for our product line?
- Are we adequately guiding and contributing to cost-reduction efforts?

Adequate appraisal of the marketing function requires involvement with the other company functions. Design, production, finance, information systems, accounting, and any other relevant functions should be included to share and impart their special points of view to the marketing appraisal. Include field sales and sales management people to impart their unique views to the appraisal process. A periodic auditing of the customer base to acquire that view of our marketing is of value to the process as well.

Marketing Organization

Areas in which we propose asking questions about the organization are:

- *Organization focus.* Is marketing organized to suit the customer's convenience or our internal convenience? Is our style of organization appropriate, clearly defined, and consistently observed? Have we considered alternative structures? Are our organization style and structure effectively integrated?

• *Adequacy in quantity and quality.* How does our present structure and staffing match up with the capabilities of the other functions of the business? For example, does our product planning capability match up with research and engineering capacity? Is our sales and service capability suitable to the production capacity of the business, and vice versa?

• *Internal work versus purchased services.* Are we doing work internally that might better be provided by outside agencies? Are we stretching our capacities or overutilizing our key people instead of going to outside providers whose expertise and availability can better serve our needs? In this regard, always factor into the evaluation the concept of "lost opportunity." If we use one of our own people on a task, what of their normal productivity are we losing? Is the division of effort between our own staff and outside services, such as advertising agencies or sales training firms, in appropriate balance?

• *Planning and strategy emphasis.* Are we striking the desired balance between current and long-term activities? Is our organization suitable to the strategies we have elected? Are sales and product development strategically compatible? Is our work planning realistic and effective?

• *Balance and relationships.* Is each marketing function given proper emphasis, or are we skewed toward or away from some? Does our structure facilitate teamwork and cooperation with other functions? Is the decision authority clearly defined within marketing and when working in concert with the other functions?

• *Supervision and control.* Is all work properly assigned and clearly understood? Is our marketing operation effective, efficient, and economical?

• *Work climate.* Does our organizational structure facilitate, or does it hinder, communications within marketing and with the other functions? Is the spirit and morale within the marketing organization good? Are there actions we can take to motivate marketing people better through organizational or personal change?

As we emphasized in Part Two of this book, our observation of marketing organizations shows at least two distinct general patterns that are troublesome.

Some companies are very reluctant to make changes and suffer along with an obsolete structure long after its appropriateness has faded with changing conditions. Others shift their structure, with major or minor modifications, so frequently that there is never a period of relative calm and thereby increased productivity.

Neither of these extremes suits customer service and needs, or the maximization of profits. The appraisal effort should aim toward a sensible balance between these two pitfalls.

Marketing Personnel

The approach to an appraisal of marketing personnel may need to include the human resources or personnel department, depending on company policy.

• *Personnel planning.* Is our current staffing adequate to accomplish our marketing objectives? Are our plans for recruiting and development of staff adequate presently and in the foreseeable future?

• *Development and training.* Do we have the in-house programs we need? Are we sending our people to outside programs where these are useful? Are we making adequate use of our senior marketing personnel to coach and develop newer people? Are our promotion policy and practice what it should be? How do our own employees view this?

• *Personnel evaluation.* Do we regularly schedule performance evaluations? Are marketing personnel contributing properly to teamwork, both within marketing and to other functions? Are our compensation practices and policies in line with industry standards? With other functions within the company? How do our employees view this?

Strategic Planning

Here we should be appraising the adequacy and functioning of the planning system of the marketing function, the quality of the plans it generates, and the results of that planning.

• *Planning system and process.* Are timely and workable plans being generated? Is marketing making adequate contributions to overall planning for the business? Are marketing plans being effectively integrated with the plans of other functions of the business? Do the other functions of the business agree with marketing's evaluation?

• *Market analysis.* Are the definitions of product lines and market segments appropriate to planning purposes? Are the definitions abreast of changing conditions? Is the growth-curve line for each product line maintained accurately and kept current? Is the intelligence-gathering system keeping ahead of planning needs?

• *Marketing objectives.* Do long-range objectives deal with increasing, holding, or decreasing sales volume, market position, and profit margins? Are short-range objectives geared to the business cycle? In a cyclical upturn, do they call for increasing share, maintaining share, or price improvement? In a turndown, do they call for holding volume, holding share, or holding profit?

• *Marketing strategy emphasis.* What is the current dominant strategy for each business segment? Are these choices still appropriate? Are they in harmony with current objectives?

• *Implementation of plans.* Are the plans adequately documented and effectively communicated? Are they accepted within the organization, or is there resistance? Have the plans been adapted to changing conditions and assumptions?

Part Three of this book is useful where a more complete appraisal is necessary.

Product System

In appraising the product system, we should judge by marketplace standards, competitive achievement, and accomplishment of stated objectives. Each product line or business segment should be analyzed.

• *Performance contribution.* Does the product system focus on customer needs and wants? How does it compare with the product systems of competitors?

• *Product planning.* Are we developing new products? Are we effective in maintaining existing product lines and introducing suitable modifications? Do we prune unsuitable or unproductive lines?

• *Product objectives and strategies.* Are we achieving market expansion with present lines by developing new features, achieving cost reductions, and lowering service costs? Are we offering new lines, serving new customers, and exploiting new technologies?

Are we increasing market share through better product performance, quality, and features? Are we contributing to increased profitability through product-line pruning, cost reduction, and price improvement where appropriate?

• *Product-related activities.* Are our packaging, general appearance, and design on a par with or ahead of our competitors'? Is adequate attention given to brand name, trademark, and labeling of our line?

• *Production scheduling.* Are our efforts in scheduling attuned to our customers' needs? Or to our sales and distribution needs? Are they as responsive as our competitors'?

Special attention must be given to interfunctional teamwork and integration of effort because of the major contributions to this area by engineering, production, finance, information systems, and other related functions.

Pricing Policy and Practices

Price formulation is a part of overall product planning. But because of the impact of pricing policy and practices on the profitability of the business, we recommend a separate appraisal of this area. Pricing appraisal should deal with individual lines as well as with the business as a whole.

• *Pricing objectives and strategies.* Are they clearly understood by all those in the organization's implementation? Have
we considered alternatives, to anticipate changing customer
and competitive situations?

• *Competitive information.* Is it current, accurate, and adequate for our pricing needs? Do we know how our customers
value our product?

• *Operating information.* Do we have adequate information
on utilization of capacity, fixed and variable costs, and other
data needed for price formulation? Have we considered the impact of price change on others of our products?

• *Price changes.* Is pricing authority clearly seen and evaluated as to the effect of changes on the business? Are we skillful
in handling price changes with our various constituencies: customers, distributors, employees, and the public?

• *Pricing effectiveness.* Are we consistent in following our
pricing strategies? Do our prices reflect the total value we deliver with our products and services? How do the sales staff and
distributors view our pricing? Do we estimate competitive bidding well in such situations? Do we sell value strongly, or are
our people accustomed to asking for price concessions?

Persuasion System

Here, analysis of each product line is desirable.

• *Focus.* Is the persuasion system focused on customer convenience, needs, and satisfaction? How does it compare with
competitors' systems?

• *Approach.* Is the persuasion approach valid for the product line? Is it harmonious with the approaches for other company products?

• *Sales force.* Is the sales force adequate in quality and size
to achieve our marketing objectives? Is there proper balance of
coverage between specialized and generalized coverage? Are
sales training needs being met for sales skills attainment, product knowledge, and support activities? Is the deployment of
sales and sales-management people in tune with opportunity?

Are compensation and incentive programs competitive and effective?

• *Market development.* Are supporting promotional tools and activities and customer-education programs adequate?

• *Promotional activities.* Is the advertising program adequate for the areas of preselling, sales support, and direct sales for each business segment? Is the sales-promotion program adequate and properly integrated with advertising output?

• *Merchandising.* Are agents, sales people, and distributors supplied with point-of-sale, demonstration, promotion, and other tools adequate to their needs? Are we monitoring the use and effectiveness of these programs at the field level?

• *Persuasion mix.* Is the mix of advertising, promotion, publicity, exhibits, demonstrations, and customer-satisfaction testimonials suitable for each product line? Are we monitoring these expenditures and programs adequately?

Failure to deploy persuasion resources and budgets in a market-sensitive and timely manner is a common and costly marketing pitfall. Too often, habit, tradition, or special pressure dictates the mix and the allocations. Changes in market conditions must also be factored into this appraisal.

Support System

As with the product and persuasion systems, we should appraise the marketing support system. We should also include the support aspects of any other functions in the company, as judged by the customer base.

• *Performance contribution.* Does the support system focus on customer satisfaction and convenience? How does it compare with the support provided by competitors?

• *Relationships.* Is the support system effectively linked to the product system, meshing with product planning and scheduling? Does it positively reinforce the message of the persuasion system? Is it deemed to be a "plus" by the customers? Are in-house support activities orchestrated with agents, distributors, and sales force so that gaps and overlaps are eliminated?

• *Physical flow of product.* Are sales forecasts and budgets precise enough to serve planning and current operations? Does production scheduling meet sales and distribution demands and the timing of customer needs? Is inventory control managed and monitored so that demand can be fulfilled in a reasonable time span? Are warehousing, shipping, and delivery systems responsive to marketplace needs?

• *Customer service.* Is service at all levels prompt, accurate, and efficient? Are proper provisions made for installation, repair, and replacement in a timely fashion? Are our quotation system, order-input facility, and complaint adjustment handling customers' needs adequately? How does the outside sales force view these functions?

• *Cost/benefit relationships.* Are we delivering support activities at sufficient value to the customer in relation to what he or she is paying for our product? How do we compare with our competition? Is our support consonant with the profit we are realizing?

Marketing Results

Here we are appraising overall marketing results for each business segment, as well as for the business as a whole.

• *Evidence of entrepreneurship.* How well have we done in identifying new business opportunities? Are we learning from our failures? What are we learning? Have we pruned products, services, markets, and distribution where appropriate? Are we managing change effectively by anticipating and taking initiative where there are shifts in markets, competition, and the environment? Are we innovating in products, services, and persuasion approaches?

• *Accuracy of forecasting.* Are general economic forecasts adequate to our needs? Can we provide forecasts of industry and competitive performance? Are our sales forecasts sufficiently precise for use in sales planning, production scheduling, facilities commitments, financial resources, and other needs of the business?

• *Marketing leadership.* Is our market position clear and appropriate for our resources and products and services? Are we meeting our goals for improvement?

• *Achievement of marketing objectives.* Are we meeting our expansion objectives? Is marketing making the maximum possible contribution through volume, pricing strategy, cost control, and other marketing tools and methods?

• *Balance between profit and growth.* Is marketing's role in achieving profit clearly defined and realistic? Is marketing's role in achieving growth clearly defined and realistic? Are the profit and growth objectives of the company compatible, and realistic from a marketing point of view?

These ten appraisal categories are a useful point of departure for an appraisal. Some questions may not be appropriate for your company or your industry. We hope that these ten serve as a stimulus for creation of your own questions and categories. We recommend rating sheets or scoring systems for an ongoing annual or periodic appraisal process.

22

A Marketing Appraisal Action Plan

Many of the action decisions reached during the appraisal process are put into plan immediately. Others require time for implementation. Regardless of the distinction, all decisions should be formally logged for follow-through.

Logging Action Items

An action log is an essential tool of the appraisal process. It will be a useful source and reference in formulating the action plan. Here are four suggested considerations in designing an action log and plan:

1. Log each item where change or improvement is called for.
2. Have a clear definition of the problem and why it warrants attention.
3. For each action area, record actions already taken, those to be pursued, and the effect expected.
4. Where future action is called for, indicate the first step, who will take it, and when. Specify a time for reviewing progress and setting subsequent steps.

Timing and Agenda for Subsequent Appraisals

In the final session of the appraisal process, consideration should be given to the frequency with which such a comprehensive evaluation is desirable. Some marketing managers have decided that this should be a continuous process, with some appraisal subjects scheduled as frequently as monthly. Others favor a more measured approach, with a major appraisal done every year or two. Many marketing managers have found it useful to maintain a file for the appraisal process and channel thoughts and ideas into it as they come to mind.

If a continuous series of appraisals is decided on, a different agenda from the ten categories proposed earlier may be in order. Three examples of suitable topics for such sessions follow.

1. *Marketing's role in the money system.* One way of looking at a business is to consider marketing's role in the money system of the business. This appraisal session would concentrate

---

The Marketing Audit

"Marketers should do an annual marketing audit. Companies bring in their accounting firm to audit their financials at the end of the year, and they ought to audit the performance of their marketing programs, too, by comparing expenses against results. The most important consideration should be the return on the marketing investment. But along the way, the company should have a professional assessment of customer satisfaction among key target groups. The assessment will help determine which decisions in the marketing mix were made correctly.

"The CEO and marketing director should have an assessment of when the overall plan achieved its stated financial and nonfinancial goals.

"And, very importantly, they ought to have an autopsy done of all the aspects of the plan that failed to meet objectives, with very specific recommendations for improving next year's performance—when the slate will be clean again."

Source: Kevin J. Clancy, chairman, Yankelovich, Clancy, Shulman, and professor of marketing, Boston University, in an interview quoted in *Business Marketing.*

on how well marketing is making its proper contributions. Here the discussion might include:

- Permitted costs—product, distribution, and support activities
- Pricing—formulation, application, conditions and terms of sale, and credit and collection
- Volume trends—results and leverage on both orders and shipments
- Sales methods—outright, time sales, rental-lease, service lease, and their effect on cash flow and profit
- Profit—measurements, emphasis on marketing's contributions

In addition to its direct influence on and participation in the money system, marketing has many opportunities for indirect influence. For example, it should be involved in research and development planning to ensure proper consideration of marketing viewpoints. It should bring forecasting influence to bear on appropriations for plant and production facilities. And marketing should influence finance to put money into programs that make sense from a marketing viewpoint.

2. *Some ideas that pay off.* Another fruitful appraisal session can be spent identifying ideas and approaches that pay off in your particular business. Some examples are:

- Market segmentation
- Product differentiation
- Selective selling
- Unique selling propositions
- Pruning products, distribution, services
- Leverage—the relative power of promotion, direct customer contact, and customer assistance in application and installation, for particular market segments
- Use of a consistent theme for all persuasion efforts
- Buying or selling market position
- Showmanship—its costs and effects

The emphasis here is on evaluating comparative merits and suitability to improve the marketing effort in the future.

3. *The big idea.* Any appraisal subject with significant impact might be called the big idea. This approach tests the creative and innovative mettle of the marketing organization. Agenda items for consideration here are:

- Finding or developing a whole new business for the company
- Introducing a new product or service
- Developing or entering a new market
- Using a sales channel unique to the competitive arena
- Adapting a marketing strategy new to the industry
- Innovating with a unique sales theme
- Creating a striking, unusual, or exotic promotion
- Providing an appealing extra customer service

Participants should be encouraged to bring to such sessions case examples from other companies or industries that illustrate the big idea at work.

Self-Appraisal Process

Marketing managers who have conducted comprehensive self-appraisal projects report many benefits from this activity. Some had fairly obvious, anticipated results; others were surprising windfalls that were equally worthwhile. Some of the benefits are that:

- Many serious and chronic marketing problems may be overlooked or shoved under the rug because of the press of daily operating demands. The appraisal gets them out into the open for attention.
- Conflicts within marketing and with other functions may be soft-pedaled because everyone is too well-mannered to talk about them. The self-appraisal process tends to generate frankness, even bluntness. Thereby the conflicts see daylight.

- Probably most importantly, though, the self-appraisal project motivates participants to come out of their provincial shells. They must take a searching look at the marketing operation as a whole—including its fundamental relationship to the whole business enterprise.

Index

181